Table of Contents

Free Gift

I am also have one valuable bonus for you - 1000 Worldwide Recipes - cookbook

Please follow this link to get instant access to your Free Cookbook: **http://booknation.top/**

Introduction

Air Fryer is a new word in modern kitchen gadgets. This tool can solve 3 the most common tasks: it helps you to save time, to cook the food in better, healthier way, and to prepare really very delightful dishes! Ths is true that Air Fryer can make the food tasty even without a big amount of fat or oils. As usual, the meal can be cooked with only 25 % of the fat (oil) that you used to add. There are no any difficulties in choosing the time of cooking – every Air Fryer has instruction on the temperature chart. That is why you can easily adjust needed temperature and time of cooking. Otherwise, it is very easy to burn the food while cooking. You should bear in mind that the food with the kitchen gadget can be cooked very fast. That is why if you do not follow the instructions of the manufacturer. Firstly, set the air fryer to 355 F for 5 minutes. After this, check if the dish is cooked – and remove or continue to cook the prepared ingredients.

The Air Fryer set contains the air fryer basket, rack, shell, and a pan or drawer. All the ingredients for the meal should be put directly in the air fryer basket.

There are no any recommendations for the amount of the oil you should add. It depends on your taste and the type of food you cook. If you follow any certain diet – you can even cook the meals without it.

The air fryer can bake, grill, and fry. For doing this, you will need to buy additional accessories/tools.

The easy way of cleaning the kitchen equipment is also very attractive feature for our modern life. There are many special detergents for the air fryer; nevertheless, it can be simply cleaned with the cloth and dish soap.

The Air Fryer food is healthy, useful, and save almost all vitamins and minerals that is impossible to do with an ordinary way of cooking. If you try it ones – you can be definitely sure you will fall in love with it!

Breakfast

Egg Cups with Bacon

Prep time: 10 minutes
Cooking time: 15 minutes
Servings: 4

Ingredients:

- 4 eggs
- 6 oz. bacon
- ¼ teaspoon salt
- ½ teaspoon dried dill
- ½ teaspoon paprika
- 1 tablespoon butter

Directions:

Beat the eggs in the mixer bowl. After this, add salt, dried dill, and paprika. Mix the egg mixture carefully with the help of the hand mixer. Then spread 4 ramekins with the butter. Slice the bacon and put it in the prepared ramekins in the shape of cups. Then pour the egg mixture in the middle of every ramekin with bacon. Set the Air Fryer to 360 F. Put the ramekins in the Air Fryer and close it. Cook the dish for 15 minutes. When the time is over – you will get tender egg mixture and little bit crunchy bacon. Remove the egg cups from the Air Fryer and serve them. Enjoy!

Nutrition: calories 319, fat 25.1, fiber 0.1, carbs 1.2, protein 21.4

Eggs in Avocado Boards

Prep time: 8 minutes
Cooking time: 15 minutes
Servings: 2

Ingredients:

- 1 avocado, pitted
- ¼ teaspoon turmeric
- ¼ teaspoon ground black pepper
- ¼ teaspoon salt
- 2 eggs
- 1 teaspoon butter
- ¼ teaspoon flax seeds

Directions:

Take the shallow bowl and combine the turmeric, ground black pepper, salt, and flax seeds together. Shake it gently to make homogeneous. After this, cut the avocado into 2 parts. Beat the eggs in the separate bowls. Sprinkle the eggs with the spice mixture. Then place the eggs in the avocado halves gently. Put the avocado boards in the Air Fryer. Set the Air Fryer to 355 F and close it. Cook the dish for 15 minutes. Open the Air Fryer after 10 minutes of cooking – if you like, the texture of the eggs you can remove them or keep cooking to make the eggs solid. Serve the breakfast immediately!

Nutrition: calories 288, fat 26, fiber 6.9, carbs 9.4, protein 7.6

Morning Ham Hash

Prep time: 10 minutes
Cooking time: 10 minutes
Servings: 3

Ingredients:

- 5 oz. Parmesan
- 10 oz. ham
- 1 tablespoon butter
- ½ onion

- 1 teaspoon ground black pepper
- 1 egg
- 1 teaspoon paprika

Directions:

Shred Parmesan cheese. Then cut the ham into the small strips. Peel the onion and dice it. Beat the egg in the bowl and whisk it with the help of the hand whisker. Add the ham strips, butter, diced onion, and butter. After this, sprinkle the mixture with the ground black pepper and paprika. Mix it up. Preheat Air Fryer to 350 F. Transfer the ham mixture into 3 ramekins and sprinkle them with the shredded Parmesan cheese. Place the ramekins in the preheated Air Fryer and cook them for 10 minutes. When the time is over – remove the ramekins from Air Fryer and mix up the ham hash with the help of the fork. Serve the dish!

Nutrition: calories 372, fat 23.7, fiber 2.1, carbs 8, protein 33.2

Cloud Eggs

Prep time: 8 minutes
Cooking time: 4 minutes
Servings: 2

Ingredients:

- 2 eggs

- 1 teaspoon butter

Directions:

Separate the eggs into the egg whites and the egg yolks. Then whisk the egg whites with the help of the hand mixer until you get strong white peaks. After this, spread the Air Fryer basket tray with the butter. Preheat the Air Fryer to 300 F. Make the medium clouds from the egg white peaks in the prepared Air Fryer basket tray. Place the basket tray in the Air Fryer and cook the cloud eggs for 2 minutes. After this, remove the basket from the Air Fryer, place the egg yolks in the center of every egg cloud, and return the basket back in the Air Fryer. Cook the dish for 2 minutes more. After this, remove the cooked dish from the basket and serve. Enjoy!

Nutrition: calories 80, fat 6.3, fiber 0, carbs 0.3, protein 5.6

Baked Bacon Egg Cups

Prep time: 10 minutes
Cooking time: 12 minutes
Servings: 2

Ingredients:
- 2 eggs
- 4 oz. bacon
- ¼ teaspoon salt
- ½ teaspoon butter
- 3 oz. Cheddar cheese, shredded
- ½ teaspoon cayenne pepper
- ½ teaspoon paprika
- 1 tablespoon chives

Directions:
Chop the bacon into the tiny pieces and sprinkle it with the salt, cayenne pepper, and paprika. Mix the chopped bacon with the help of the fingertips. After this, spread the ramekins with the butter and beat the eggs there. Add the shredded cheese and chives. After this, put the chopped bacon over the chives. Put the ramekins in the Air Fryer basket and preheat the air fryer to 360 F. Put the air fryer basket with the ramekins in the air fryer and cook the breakfast for 12 minutes. When the time is over – remove the ramekins from the air fryer and chill them little. Remove the bacon egg cups from the ramekins carefully. Enjoy!

Nutrition: calories 553, fat 43.3, fiber 0.4, carbs 2.3, protein 37.3

Cauliflower Fritters

Prep time: 10 minutes
Cooking time: 15 minutes
Servings: 4

Ingredients:
- 1 tablespoon dried dill
- 1 egg
- 1 teaspoon salt
- 10 oz. cauliflower
- 1 tablespoon almond flour
- 1 teaspoon olive oil
- 1 tablespoon parsley
- ½ teaspoon ground white pepper

Directions:
Wash the cauliflower carefully and chop it into the small pieces. Then place the cauliflower in the blender and blend it well. Beat the egg in the cauliflower mixture and continue to blend it for 1 minute more. After this, transfer the blended cauliflower mixture in the bowl. Sprinkle it with the salt, dried dill, almond flour, parsley, and ground white pepper. Mix it up carefully with the help of the spoon. Preheat the air fryer to 355 F. Then sprinkle the air fryer basket tray with the olive oil. Make the fritters from the cauliflower mixture and put them in the air fryer basket tray. Close the air fryer and cook the fritters for 8 minutes. After this, turn the fritters to another side and cook them for 7 minutes more. When the fritters are cooked – serve them hot! Enjoy!

Nutrition: calories 54, fat 3.1, fiber 2.1, carbs 4.8, protein 3.3

Egg-Meat Rolls

Prep time: 15 minutes
Cooking time: 8 minute
Servings: 6

Ingredients:
- ½ cup almond flour
- ¼ cup water
- 1 teaspoon salt
- 1 egg

- 7 oz. ground beef
- 1 teaspoon paprika
- 1 teaspoon ground black pepper
- 1 tablespoon olive oil

Directions:
Preheat the water until it starts to boil. Then combine the almond flour with the salt and stir it. Add the boiling water and whisk it carefully until the mixture is homogenous. Then knead the smooth and soft dough. Leave the dough. Meanwhile, combine the ground beef with the paprika and ground black pepper. Mix the mixture up and transfer it to the pan. Roast the meat mixture for 5 minutes on the medium heat. Stir it frequently. After this beat the egg in the meat mixture and scramble it. Cook the ground beef mixture for 4 minutes more. Then roll the dough and cut it into the 6 squares. Put the ground beef mixture in the every square. Roll the squares to make the dough sticks. Sprinkle the dough sticks with the olive oil. After this, put the prepared dough sticks in the air fryer basket. Preheat the air fryer to 350 F and put the egg-meat rolls there. Cook the dish for 8 minutes. When the egg-meat rolls are cooked – transfer them directly to the serving plates. Enjoy!

Nutrition: calories 150, fat 9.6, fiber 1.2, carbs 2.5, protein 13

Classic Egg Rolls

Prep time: 10 minutes
Cooking time: 8 minutes
Servings: 4

Ingredients:
- 6 tablespoon coconut flour
- ½ teaspoon salt
- 1 teaspoon paprika
- 1 teaspoon butter

- 4 eggs
- 1 teaspoon chives
- 1 tablespoon olive oil
- 2 tablespoon water, boiled, hot

Directions:
Put the coconut flour in the bowl. Add salt and hot boiled water. Mix it up and knead the soft dough. After this, leave the dough to rest. Meanwhile, crack the eggs into the bowl. Add the chives and paprika. Whisk it up with the help of the hand whisker. Then toss the butter in the pan and preheat it well. Pour the egg mixture in the melted butter in the shape of the pancake. Then cook the egg pancake for 1 minute from the each side. After this, remove the cooked egg pancake and chop it. Roll the prepared dough and cut it into the 4 squares. Put the chopped eggs in the dough squares and roll them in the shape of the sticks. Then brush the egg rolls with the olive oil. Preheat the air fryer to 355 F. Put the egg rolls in the basket and transfer the basket in the air fryer. Cook the dish for 8 minutes. When the time is over the rolls should get light brown color. Serve the dish hot. Enjoy!

Nutrition: calories 148, fat 10, fiber 4.7, carbs 8.2, protein 7.1

Breakfast Sausages

Prep time: 15 minutes
Cooking time: 12 minutes
Servings: 6

Ingredients:

- 7 oz. ground chicken
- 7 oz. ground pork
- 1 teaspoon minced garlic
- 1 teaspoon salt
- ½ teaspoon nutmeg
- 1 teaspoon olive oil
- 1 tablespoon almond flour
- 1 egg
- 1 teaspoon chili flakes
- 1 teaspoon ground coriander

Directions:

Combine the ground chicken and ground pork together in the bowl. Beat the egg in the mixture. Then mix it up with the help of the spoon. After this, sprinkle the meat mixture with the minced garlic, salt, nutmeg, almond flour, chili flakes, and ground coriander. Mix it up to make the smooth texture of the ground meat. Preheat the air fryer to 360 F. Make the medium sausages from the ground meat mixture. Spray the air fryer basket tray with the olive oil inside. Then place the prepared sausages in the air fryer basket and place it in the air fryer. Cook the sausages for 6 minutes. After this, turn the sausages into the second side and cook them for 6 minutes more. When the time is over and the sausages are cooked – let them chill for a while. Serve and taste!

Nutrition: calories 156, fat 7.5, fiber 0.6, carbs 1.3, protein 20.2

Breakfast Blackberry Muffins

Prep time: 15 minutes
Cooking time: 10 minutes
Servings: 5

Ingredients:

- 1 teaspoon apple cider vinegar
- 1 cup almond flour
- 4 tablespoon butter
- 6 tablespoon almond milk
- 1 teaspoon baking soda
- 3 oz. blackberry
- ½ teaspoon salt
- 3 teaspoon stevia
- 1 teaspoon vanilla extract

Directions:

Put the almond flour in the mixing bowl. Add the baking soda, salt, stevia, and vanilla extract. After this, add butter, almond milk, and apple cider vinegar. Smash the blackberries gently and add them to the almond flour mixture. Stir it carefully with the help of the fork until the mass is homogeneous. After this, leave the muffin mixture for 5 minutes in warm place. Meanwhile, preheat the air fryer to 400 F. Prepare the muffin forms. Pour the dough in the muffin forms. Fill only ½ part of every muffin form. When the air fryer is preheated – put the muffing forms with the filling in the air fryer basket. Close the air fryer. Cook the muffins for 10 minutes. When the time is over – remove the muffins from the air fryer basket. Chill them until they are warm. Serve them and enjoy!

Nutrition: calories 165, fat 16.4, fiber 1.9, carbs 4, protein 2

Light Egg Soufflé

Prep time: 8 minutes
Cooking time: 8 minutes
Servings: 2

Ingredients:

- 2 eggs
- 2 tablespoon heavy cream
- 1 tablespoon dried parsley
- ¼ teaspoon ground chili pepper
- ¼ teaspoon salt

Directions:

Preheat the air fryer to 391 F. Meanwhile, crack the eggs into the bowl and add the heavy cream. Whisk the mixture carefully until you get the smooth liquid texture. After this, sprinkle the egg mixture with the dried parsley, ground chili pepper, and salt. Mix it up with the help of the spoon. Then take 2 ramekins and pour the soufflé mixture there. Place the ramekins in the air fryer basket and cook for 8 minutes. When the time is over and the soufflé is cooked – remove the ramekins from the air fryer basket and chill for 2-3 minutes. Serve the dish and enjoy!

Nutrition: calories 116, fat 9.9, fiber 0.1, carbs 0.9, protein 5.9

Chia Pudding

Prep time: 10 minutes
Cooking time: 4 minutes
Servings: 7

Ingredients:

- 1 cup chia seeds
- 1 cup coconut milk
- 1 teaspoon stevia
- 1 tablespoon coconut
- 1 teaspoon butter

Directions:

Take the small ramekins and put the chia seeds there. Add the coconut milk and stevia. Stir the mixture gently with the help of the teaspoon. After this, add coconut and butter. Place the chia seeds pudding in the air fryer basket tray and preheat the air fryer to 360 F. Cook the chia pudding for 4 minutes. When the time is over – remove the ramekins with the chia pudding from the air fryer and chill it for 4 minutes. After this, stir every chia pudding serving with the help of the teaspoon and serve it. Enjoy!

Nutrition: calories 204, fat 16.4, fiber 10.2, carbs 12.2, protein 4.8

Keto Morning Pizza

Prep time: 10 minutes
Cooking time: 11 minutes
Servings: 6

Ingredients:

- 6 oz. Cheddar cheese, shredded
- 5 oz. Parmesan cheese, shredded
- 1 tomato
- ¼ onion
- 1 teaspoon paprika
- ½ teaspoon dried oregano
- ½ teaspoon salt
- ½ cup almond flour
- 1 egg
- 4 tablespoon water
- 1 teaspoon olive oil

Directions:

Beat the egg in the bowl and whisk it with the help of the hand whisker. After this, add the almond flour and water. Mix the mixture up carefully and after this knead the non-sticky dough. Then roll the dough into the thin circle. Preheat the air fryer to 355 F. Spray the air fryer basket tray with the olive oil and place the pizza crust there. Cook it for 1 minute. After this, remove the air fryer basket tray from the air fryer. Slice the tomato and dice the onion. Sprinkle the pizza crust with the diced onion and sliced tomato. Then put the shredded Cheddar cheese and Parmesan cheese over the sliced tomatoes. Sprinkle the pizza with salt, paprika, and dried oregano. Place the pizza back in the air fryer and cook it for 10 minutes. When the time is over and the pizza is cooked – slice it into the servings and serve!

Nutrition: calories 226, fat 17.2, fiber 0.7, carbs 2.9, protein 16.3

Buffalo Cauliflower

Prep time: 10 minutes
Cooking time: 15 minutes
Servings: 5

Ingredients:

- 8 oz. cauliflower
- 6 tablespoon almond flour
- 1 teaspoon chili pepper
- 1 teaspoon cayenne pepper
- 1 teaspoon ground black pepper
- 1 tomato
- 1 teaspoon minced garlic
- ½ teaspoon salt
- 1 teaspoon olive oil

Directions:

Wash the cauliflower carefully and separate it into the medium florets. Sprinkle the cauliflower florets with the salt. After this, chop the tomato roughly and transfer it to the blender. Blend it well. Then add the chili pepper, cayenne pepper, ground black pepper, and minced garlic. Blend the mixture. Then preheat the air fryer to 350 F. Sprinkle the air fryer basket with the olive oil inside. Sprinkle the cauliflower florets with the blended tomato mixture generously. After this, coat the cauliflower florets in the almond flour. Place the coated cauliflower florets in the air fryer basket and cook the dish for 15 minutes. Shake the cauliflower florets every 4 minutes. When the cauliflower is cooked – it will have light brown color. Transfer it to the serving plates. Enjoy!

Nutrition: calories 217, fat 17.9, fiber 5.1, carbs 10.8, protein 8.4

Pork Breakfast Sticks

Prep time: 15 minutes
Cooking time: 10 minutes
Servings: 4

Ingredients:

- 1 teaspoon dried basil
- ¼ teaspoon ground ginger
- 1 teaspoon nutmeg
- 1 teaspoon oregano
- 1 teaspoon apple cider vinegar
- 1 teaspoon paprika
- 10 oz. pork fillet
- ½ teaspoon salt
- 1 tablespoon olive oil
- 5 oz. Parmesan, shredded

Directions:

Cut the pork fillet into the thick strips. Then combine the ground ginger, nutmeg, oregano, paprika, and salt in the shallow bowl. Stir it. After this, sprinkle the pork strips with the spice mixture. Sprinkle the meat with the apple cider vinegar. Preheat the air fryer to 380 F. Sprinkle the air fryer basket with the olive oil inside and place the pork strips (sticks) there. Cook the dish for 5 minutes. After this, turn the pork sticks to another side and cook for 4 minutes more. Then cover the pork sticks with the shredded Parmesan and cook the dish for 1 minute more. Remove the pork sticks from the air fryer and serve them immediately. The cheese should be soft during the serving. Enjoy!

Nutrition: calories 315, fat 20.4, fiber 0.5, carbs 2.2, protein 31.3

Keto Bacon

Prep time: 8 minutes
Cooking time: 10 minutes
Servings: 4

Ingredients:

- 8 oz. bacon
- ½ teaspoon dried oregano
- ½ teaspoon salt
- ½ teaspoon ground black pepper
- ½ teaspoon ground thyme
- 4 oz. Cheddar cheese

Directions:

Slice the bacon and rub it with the dried oregano, salt, ground black pepper, and ground thyme from the each side. Leave the bacon for 2-3 minutes to make it soak the spices. Meanwhile, preheat the air fryer to 360 F. Place the sliced bacon in the air fryer rack and cook it for 5 minutes. After this, turn the sliced bacon to another side and cook it for 5 minutes more. Meanwhile, shred Cheddar cheese. When the bacon is cooked – sprinkle it with the shredded cheese and cook for 30 seconds more. Then transfer the cooked bacon to the plates. Enjoy the breakfast immediately!

Nutrition: calories 423, fat 33.1, fiber 0.2, carbs 1.5, protein 28.1

Cheese Tots

Prep time: 12 minutes
Cooking time: 3 minutes
Servings: 5

Ingredients:
- 8 oz. mozzarella balls
- 1 egg
- ½ cup coconut flakes
- ½ cup almond flour
- 1 teaspoon thyme
- 1 teaspoon ground black pepper
- 1 teaspoon paprika

Directions:
Beat the egg in the bowl and whisk it. After this, combine the coconut flour with the thyme, ground black pepper, and paprika. Stir it carefully. Then sprinkle Mozzarella balls with the coconut flakes. After this, transfer the balls to the whisked egg mixture. Then coat them in the almond flour mixture. Put Mozzarella balls in the freezer for 5 minutes. Meanwhile, preheat the air fryer to 400 F. Put the frozen cheese balls in the preheated air fryer and cook them for 3 minutes. When the time is over – remove the cheese tots from the air fryer basket and chill them for 2 minutes. Serve the dish!

Nutrition: calories 166, fat 12.8, fiber 1.4, carbs 2.8, protein 9.5

Sausage Balls

Prep time: 10 minutes
Cooking time: 8 minutes
Servings: 5

Ingredients:
- 8 oz. ground chicken
- 1 egg white
- 1 tablespoon dried parsley
- ½ teaspoon salt
- ½ teaspoon ground black pepper
- 2 tablespoon almond flour
- 1 tablespoon olive oil
- 1 teaspoon paprika

Directions:
Whisk the egg white and combine it with the ground chicken. Sprinkle the chicken mixture with the dried parsley and salt. After this, add the ground black pepper and paprika. Stir the mass carefully using the spoon. Then make the hands wet and make the small balls from the ground chicken mixture. Sprinkle every sausage ball with the almond flour. Preheat the air fryer to 380 F. Then spray the air fryer basket tray with the olive oil inside and put the sausage balls there. Cook the dish for 8 minutes. You can turn the balls into another side during the cooking to get the brown color of the each side. Transfer the cooked sausage balls in the serving plates. Enjoy!

Nutrition: calories 180, fat 11.8, fiber 1.5, carbs 2.9, protein 16.3

Tofu Scramble

Prep time: 15 minutes
Cooking time: 20 minutes
Servings: 5

Ingredients:

- 10 oz tofu cheese
- 2 eggs
- 1 teaspoon chives
- 1 tablespoon apple cider vinegar
- ½ teaspoon salt
- 1 teaspoon ground white pepper
- ¼ teaspoon ground coriander

Directions:

Shred tofu cheese and sprinkle it with the apple cider vinegar, salt, ground white pepper, and ground coriander. Mix it up and leave for 10 minutes to marinate. Meanwhile, preheat the air fryer to 370 F. Then transfer the marinated shredded tofu cheese in the air fryer basket tray and cook the cheese for 13 minutes. Meanwhile, beat the eggs in the bowl and whisk them. When the time is over – pour the egg mixture in the shredded tofu cheese and stir it with the help of the spatula well. When the eggs start to be firm – place the air fryer basket tray in the air fryer and cook the dish for 7 minutes more. After this, remove the cooked meal from the air fryer basket tray and serve it. Enjoy!

Nutrition: calories 109, fat 6.7, fiber 1.4, carbs 2.9, protein 11.2

Hemp Seeds Porridge

Prep time: 10 minutes
Cooking time: 15 minutes
Servings: 3

Ingredients:

- 2 tablespoon flax seeds
- 4 tablespoon hemp seeds
- 1 tablespoon butter
- ¼ teaspoon salt
- 1 teaspoon stevia
- 7 tablespoon almond milk
- ½ teaspoon ground ginger

Directions:

Place the flax seeds and hemp seeds in the air fryer basket. Sprinkle the seeds with the salt and ground ginger. Combine the almond milk and stevia together. Stir the liquid and pour it in the seeds mixture. After this, add butter. Preheat the air fryer to 370 F and cook the hemp seeds porridge for 15 minutes. Stir it carefully after 10 minutes of cooking. When the time is over – remove the hem porridge from the air fryer basket tray and chill it for 3 minutes. Transfer the Hemp Seeds porridge in the serving bowls. Enjoy!

Nutrition: calories 196, fat 18.2, fiber 2.4, carbs 4.2, protein 5.1

Bacon Scrambled Eggs

Prep time: 10 minutes
Cooking time: 10 minutes
Servings: 4

Ingredients:

- 6 oz. bacon
- 4 eggs
- 5 tablespoon heavy cream
- 1 tablespoon butter
- 1 teaspoon paprika
- ½ teaspoon nutmeg
- 1 teaspoon salt
- 1 teaspoon ground black pepper

Directions:

Chop the bacon into the small pieces and sprinkle it with salt. Stir the bacon gently and put in the air fryer basket. Cook the chopped bacon in the preheated to 360 F air fryer for 5 minutes. Meanwhile, beat the eggs in the bowl and whisk them using the hand whisker. Sprinkle the whisked egg mixture with the paprika, nutmeg, and ground black pepper. Whisk egg mixture gently again. When the time is over – toss the butter in the chopped bacon and pour the egg mixture. Add the heavy cream and cook it for 2 minutes. After this, stir the mixture with the help of the spatula until you get the scrambled eggs and cook the dish for 3 minutes more. Then transfer the cooked bacon scrambled eggs in the serving plates. Enjoy!

Nutrition: calories 387, fat 32.1, fiber 0.4, carbs 2.3, protein 21.9

Delightful Breakfast Hash

Prep time: 8 minutes
Cooking time: 8 minutes
Servings: 4

Ingredients:

- 1 zucchini
- 7 oz. bacon, cooked
- 4 oz. Cheddar cheese
- 2 tablespoon butter
- 1 teaspoon salt
- 1 teaspoon ground black pepper
- 1 teaspoon paprika
- 1 teaspoon cilantro
- 1 teaspoon ground thyme

Directions:

Chop the zucchini into the small cubes and sprinkle it with the salt, ground black pepper, paprika, cilantro, and ground thyme. Preheat the air fryer to 400 F and toss the butter in the air fryer basket tray. Melt it and add the zucchini cubes. Cook the zucchini for 5 minutes. Meanwhile, shred Cheddar cheese. When the time is over – shake the zucchini cubes carefully and add the cooked bacon. Sprinkle the zucchini mixture with the shredded cheese and cook it for 3 minutes more. When the time is over – transfer the breakfast hash in the serving bowls and stir. Enjoy!

Nutrition: calories 445, fat 36.1, fiber 1, carbs 3.5, protein 26.3

Cheddar Soufflé with Greens

Prep time: 10 minutes
Cooking time: 8 minutes
Servings: 4

Ingredients:

- 5 oz. Cheddar cheese, shredded
- 3 eggs
- 4 tablespoon heavy cream
- 1 tablespoon chives
- 1 tablespoon dill
- 1 teaspoon parsley
- ½ teaspoon ground thyme

Directions:

Crack the eggs into the bowl and whisk them carefully. After this, add the heavy cream and whisk it for 10 seconds more. Then add the chives, dill, parsley, and ground thyme. Sprinkle the egg mixture with the shredded cheese and stir it. Transfer the egg mixture in 4 ramekins and put the ramekins in the air fryer basket. Preheat the air fryer to 390 F and cook the soufflé for 8 minutes. When the time is over and the soufflé is cooked – chill it well. Enjoy!

Nutrition: calories 244, fat 20.6, fiber 0.2, carbs 1.7, protein 13.5

Bacon Biscuits

Prep time: 15 minutes
Cooking time: 10 minutes
Servings: 6

Ingredients:

- 1 egg
- 4 oz. bacon, cooked
- 1 cup almond flour
- ½ teaspoon baking soda
- 1 tablespoon apple cider vinegar
- 3 tablespoon butter
- 4 tablespoon heavy cream
- 1 teaspoon dried oregano

Directions:

Beat the egg in the bowl and whisk it. Chop the cooked bacon into the small cubes and add it in the whisked egg. Then sprinkle the mixture with the baking soda and apple cider vinegar. Add the heavy cream and dried oregano. Stir it. After this, add butter and almond flour. Mix it up with the help of the hand mixer. When you get the smooth and liquid batter – the dough is cooked. Preheat the air fryer to 400 F. Pour the batter dough into the muffin molds. When the air fryer is preheated – put the muffin forms in the air fryer basket and cook them for 10 minutes. When the time is over and the muffins are prepared – remove them from the air fryer. Chill the muffins till the room temperature. Serve!

Nutrition: calories 226, fat 20.5, fiber 0.6, carbs 1.8, protein 9.2

Keto Frittata

Prep time: 10 minutes
Cooking time: 15 minutes
Servings: 6

Ingredients:

- 6 eggs
- 1/3 cup heavy cream
- 1 tomato
- 1/2 onion
- 1 tablespoon butter
- 1 teaspoon salt
- 1 tablespoon dried oregano
- 6 oz. Parmesan
- 1 teaspoon chili pepper

Directions:

Beat the eggs in the air fryer basket tray and whisk them with the help of the hand whisker. After this, chop the tomato and dice the onion. Add the vegetables to the egg mixture. Then pour the heavy cream. Sprinkle the liquid mixture with the butter, salt, dried oregano, and chili pepper. Then shred Parmesan cheese and add it to the mixture too. Sprinkle the mixture with the silicone spatula. Preheat the air fryer to 375 F and cook the frittata for 15 minutes. When the time is over – transfer frittata in the serving plates. Enjoy!

Nutrition: calories 202, fat 15, fiber 0.7, carbs 3.4, protein 15.1

Liver Pate

Prep time: 10 minutes
Cooking time: 10 minutes
Servings: 7

Ingredients:

- 1-pound chicken liver
- 1 teaspoon salt
- 4 tablespoon butter
- 1 cup water
- 1 teaspoon ground black pepper
- 1 onion
- ½ teaspoon dried cilantro

Directions:

Chop the chicken liver roughly and place it in the air fryer basket tray. Then peel the onion and dice it. Pour the water in the air fryer basket tray and add the diced onion. Preheat the air fryer to 360 F and cook the chicken liver for 10 minutes. When the time is over – strain the chicken liver mixture to discard it from the liquid. Transfer the chicken liver mixture into the blender. Add the butter, ground black pepper, and dried cilantro. Blend the mixture till you get the pate texture. Then transfer the liver pate in the bowl and serve it immediately or keep in the fridge. Enjoy!

Nutrition: calories 173, fat 10.8, fiber 0.4, carbs 2.2, protein 16.1

Scrambled Pancake Hash

Prep time: 7 minutes
Cooking time: 9 minutes
Servings: 7

Ingredients:

- 1 teaspoon baking soda
- 1 tablespoon apple cider vinegar
- 1 teaspoon salt
- 1 teaspoon ground ginger
- 1 cup coconut flour
- 5 tablespoon butter
- 1 egg
- ¼ cup heavy cream

Directions:

Combine the baking soda, salt, ground ginger, and flour in the bowl. Take the separate bowl and crack the egg there. Add butter and heavy cream. Use the hand mixer and mix the liquid mixture well. Then combine the dry mixture and liquid mixture together and stir it until it is smooth. Preheat the air fryer to 400 F. Then pour the pancake mixture into the air fryer basket tray. Cook the pancake hash for 4 minutes. After this, scramble the pancake hash well and keep cooking it for 5 minutes more. When the dish is cooked – transfer it to the serving plates and serve only hot. Taste it!

Nutrition: calories 178, fat 13.3, fiber 6.9, carbs 10.7, protein 4.4

Meatloaf Slices

Prep time: 10 minutes
Cooking time: 20 minutes
Servings: 6

Ingredients:

- 8 oz. ground pork
- 7 oz. ground beef
- 1 onion
- 1 egg
- 1 tablespoon almond flour
- 1 tablespoon chives
- 1 teaspoon salt
- 1 teaspoon cayenne pepper
- 1 tablespoon dried oregano
- 1 teaspoon butter
- 1 teaspoon olive oil

Directions:

Beat the egg in the big bowl. Add the ground beef and ground pork. After this, add the almond flour, chives, salt, cayenne pepper, dried oregano, and butter. Peel the onion and dice it. Put the diced onion in the ground meat mixture. Use the hands to make the homogeneous meatloaf mixture. Preheat the air fryer to 350 F. Make the meatloaf form from the ground meat mixture. Sprinkle the air fryer basket with the olive oil inside and put the meatloaf there. Cook the meatloaf for 20 minutes. When the time is over – let the meatloaf chill little. Slice it and serve. Enjoy!

Nutrition: calories 176, fat 2.2, fiber 1.3, carbs 3.4, protein 22.2

Flax Meal Porridge

Prep time: 5 minutes
Cooking time: 8 minutes
Servings: 4

Ingredients:

- 2 tablespoon sesame seeds
- 4 tablespoon chia seeds
- 1 cup almond milk
- 3 tablespoon flax meal
- 1 teaspoon stevia
- 1 tablespoon butter
- ½ teaspoon vanilla extract

Directions:

Preheat the air fryer to 375 F. Put the sesame seeds, chia seeds, almond milk, flax meal, stevia, and butter in the air fryer basket tray. Add the vanilla extract and cook the porridge doe 8 minutes. When the time is over – stir the porridge carefully and leave it for 5 minutes to rest. Then transfer the meal ёin the serving bowls or ramekins. Enjoy!

Nutrition: calories 298, fat 26.7, fiber 9.4, carbs 13.3, protein 6.2

No Bun Bacon Burger

Prep time: 10 minutes
Cooking time: 8 minutes
Servings: 2

Ingredients:

- ½ tomato
- ½ cucumber
- ½ onion
- 8 oz. ground beef
- 4 oz. bacon, cooked
- 1 egg
- 1 teaspoon butter
- 2 oz. lettuce leaves
- 1 teaspoon ground black pepper
- ½ teaspoon salt
- 1 teaspoon olive oil
- ½ teaspoon minced garlic

Directions:

Beat the egg in the bowl and add the ground beef. Chop the cooked bacon and add it to the ground beef mixture. After this, add the butter, ground black pepper, salt, and minced garlic. Mix it up carefully and make the burgers. Preheat the oven to 370 F. Spray the air fryer basket with the olive oil inside and place the burgers there. Cook the burgers for 8 minutes on the each side. Meanwhile, slice the onion, cucumber, and tomato finely. Place the tomato, cucumber, and onion on the lettuce leaves. When the burgers are cooked – let them chill until the room temperature and place them over the vegetables. Serve the dish!

Nutrition: calories 618, fat 37.4, fiber 1.6, carbs 8.6, protein 59.4

Bacon Omelette

Prep time: 10 minutes
Cooking time: 13 minutes
Servings: 6

Ingredients:

- 6 eggs
- ¼ cup almond milk
- ½ teaspoon turmeric
- ½ teaspoon salt
- 1 tablespoon dried dill
- 4 oz. bacon
- 1 teaspoon butter

Directions:

Beat the egg in the mixer bowl and add almond milk. Mix up the mixture with the help of the mixer until it is smooth. Add the turmeric, salt, and dried dill. Then slice the bacon. Preheat the air fryer to 360 F and put the sliced bacon in the air fryer basket tray. Cook the bacon for 5 minutes. After this, turn the bacon into another side and pour the egg mixture over it. Cook the omelet for 8 minutes more. When the time is over and the omelet is cooked – transfer it to the plate and slice into the servings. Enjoy!

Nutrition: calories 196, fat 15.3, fiber 0.3, carbs 1.6, protein 12.9

Egg Butter

Prep time: 10 minutes
Cooking time: 17 minutes
Servings: 4

Ingredients:

- 4 eggs
- 4 tablespoon butter
- 1 teaspoon salt

Directions:

Cover the air fryer basket with the foil and place the eggs there. Then transfer the air fryer basket in the air fryer and cook the eggs for 17 minutes at 320 F. When the time is over – remove the cooked eggs from the air fryer basket and put them in the cold water to make them chill. After this, peel the eggs and chop them finely. Then combine the chopped eggs with the butter and add salt. Mix it up until you get the spread texture. Serve the egg butter with the keto almond bread. Enjoy!

Nutrition: calories 164, fat 8.5, fiber 3, carbs 21.67, protein 3

Breakfast Coconut Porridge

Prep time: 10 minutes
Cooking time: 7 minutes
Servings: 4

Ingredients:

- 1 cup coconut milk
- 3 tablespoon blackberries
- ¼ teaspoon salt
- 3 tablespoon coconut flakes
- 5 tablespoon chia seeds
- 1 teaspoon ground cinnamon
- 1 teaspoon butter
- 2 tablespoon walnuts

Directions:

Pour the coconut milk in the air fryer basket tray. Add the salt, coconut flakes, chia seeds, ground cinnamon, and butter. Crush the walnuts and add them in the air fryer basket tray too. Then sprinkle the mixture with salt. Mash the blackberries with the help of the fork and add them in the air fryer basket tray too. Cook the porridge at 375 F for 7 minutes. When the time is over – remove the air fryer basket from the air fryer and let sit for 5 minutes to rest. Then stir the porridge carefully with the help of the wooden spoon and serve. Enjoy!

Nutrition: calories 279, fat 24.6, fiber 9.1, carbs 13.3, protein 5.7

Mushroom Omelet

Prep time: 10 minutes
Cooking time: 12 minutes
Servings: 9

Ingredients:

- 1 tablespoon flax seeds
- 7 eggs
- ½ cup cream cheese
- 4 oz. white mushrooms
- 1 teaspoon olive oil
- 1 teaspoon ground black pepper
- ½ teaspoon paprika
- ¼ teaspoon salt

Directions:

Slice the mushrooms and sprinkle them with the salt, paprika, and ground black pepper. Preheat the air fryer to 400 F. Spray the air fryer basket tray with olive oil inside and place the sliced mushrooms there. Cook the mushrooms for 3 minutes. Stir them carefully after 2 minutes of cooking. Meanwhile, beat the eggs in the bowl. Add the cream cheese and flax seeds. Mix the egg mixture up carefully until you get the smooth texture. Then pour the omelet mixture into the air fryer basket tray over the mushrooms. Stir the omelet gently and cook it for 7 minutes more. When the time is over – remove the cooked omelet from the air fryer basket tray using the wooden spatula. Slice it into the servings. Enjoy!

Nutrition: calories 106, fat 8.7, fiber 0.4, carbs 1.5, protein 5.9

Western Omelette

Prep time: 10 minutes
Cooking time: 10 minutes
Servings: 4

Ingredients:
- 1 green pepper
- ½ onion
- 5 eggs
- 3 tablespoon cream cheese
- 1 teaspoon olive oil
- 1 teaspoon dried cilantro
- 1 teaspoon dried oregano
- 1 teaspoon butter
- 3 oz. Parmesan, shredded

Directions:

Beat the eggs in the bowl and whisk them well. Sprinkle the whisked eggs with the cream cheese, dried cilantro, and dried oregano. Add shredded Parmesan and butter and mix the egg mixture up. Preheat the air fryer to 360 F. Pour the egg mixture into the air fryer basket tray and place it in the air fryer. Cook the omelet for 10 minutes. Meanwhile, chop the green pepper and dice the onion. Pour the olive oil in the skillet and preheat it well. Then add the chopped green pepper and roast it for 3 minutes on the medium heat. Then add the diced onion and cook it for 5 minutes more. Stir the vegetables frequently. After this, remove the cooked omelet from the air fryer basket tray and place it on the plate. Add the roasted vegetables and serve it. Enjoy!

Nutrition: calories 204, fat 14.9, fiber 1, carbs 4.3, protein 14.8

Keto Bread-Free Sandwich

Prep time: 10 minutes
Cooking time: 10 minutes
Servings: 2

Ingredients:
- 2 slices Cheddar cheese
- 6 oz. ground chicken
- 1 teaspoon tomato puree
- 1 teaspoon cayenne pepper
- 1 egg
- ½ teaspoon salt
- 1 tablespoon dried dill
- ½ teaspoon olive oil
- 2 lettuce leaves

Directions:

Combine the ground chicken with the cayenne pepper and salt. Add the dried dill and stir it. Then beat the egg in the ground chicken mixture and stir it well with the help of the spoon. After this, make 2 medium burgers from the ground chicken mixture. Preheat the air fryer to 380 F. Spray the air fryer basket tray with the olive oil and place the ground chicken burgers there. Cook the chicken burgers for 10 minutes. Turn the burgers to another side after 6 minutes of cooking. When the time is over – transfer the cooked chicken burgers in the lettuce leaves. Sprinkle them with the tomato puree and cover with Cheddar slices. Serve it!

Nutrition: calories 324, fat 19.2, fiber 0.5, carbs 2.3, protein 34.8

Seed Porridge

Prep time: 7 minutes
Cooking time: 12 minutes
Servings: 3

Ingredients:
- 1 tablespoon butter
- 3 tablespoon chia seeds
- 3 tablespoon sesame seeds
- ¼ teaspoon salt
- 1 egg
- 1/3 cup heavy cream
- ¼ teaspoon nutmeg

Directions:

Place the butter in the air fryer basket tray. Add chia seeds, sesame seeds, heavy cream, salt, and nutmeg. Stir it gently. Then beat the egg in the mug and whisk it with the fork. Add the whisked egg in the air fryer basket tray too. Stir the mixture with the help of the wooden spatula. After this, preheat the air fryer to 375 F. Place the air fryer basket tray in the air fryer and cook the porridge for 12 minutes. Stir it 3 times during the cooking. Then remove the porridge from the air fryer basket tray immediately. Serve it hot!

Nutrition: calories 275, fat 22.5, fiber 9.7, carbs 13.2, protein 7.9

Minced Beef Keto Sandwich

Prep time: 11 minutes
Cooking time: 16 minutes
Servings: 2

Ingredients:
- 6 oz. minced beef
- ½ avocado pitted
- ½ tomato
- ½ teaspoon chili flakes
- 1/3 teaspoon salt
- ½ teaspoon ground black pepper
- 1 teaspoon olive oil
- 1 teaspoon flax seeds
- 4 lettuce leaves

Directions:

Combine the minced beef with the chili flakes and salt. Add flax seeds and stir the meat mixture with the help of the fork. Preheat the air fryer to 370 F. Pour the olive oil in the air fryer basket tray. Make 2 burgers from the beef mixture and place them in the air fryer basket tray. Cook the burgers for 8 minutes on the each side. Meanwhile, slice the tomato and avocado. Separate the sliced ingredients into 2 servings. Place the avocado and tomato on 2 lettuce leaves. Then add the cooked minced beef burgers. Serve the sandwiches only hot. Enjoy!

Nutrition: calories 292, fat 17.9, fiber 4.1, carbs 5.9, protein 27.2

Keto Spinach Quiche

Prep time: 15 minutes
Cooking time: 21 minutes
Servings: 6

Ingredients:

- ½ cup almond flour
- 4 tablespoon water, boiled
- 1 teaspoon salt
- 1 cup spinach
- ¼ cup cream cheese
- ½ onion
- 1 teaspoon ground black pepper
- 3 eggs
- 6 oz. Cheddar cheese, shredded
- 1 teaspoon olive oil

Directions:

Combine the water with the almond flour and add salt. Mix the mixture up and knead the non-sticky soft dough. Then spray the air fryer basket tray with the olive oil inside. Set the air fryer to 375 F and preheat it. Roll the dough and place it in the air fryer basket tray in the shape of the crust. After this, put the air fryer basket tray in the air fryer and cook it for 5 minutes. Meanwhile, chop the spinach and combine it with the cream cheese and ground black pepper. Dice the onion and add it to the spinach mixture. Stir it carefully. Beat the eggs in the bowl and whisk them. When the time is over and quiche crust is cooked – transfer the spinach filling in it. Sprinkle the filling with the shredded cheese and pour the whisked eggs. Then set the air fryer to 350 F and cook the quiche for 7 minutes. Then reduce the heat to 300 F and cook the quiche for 9 minutes more. Let the cooked quiche chill well and cut it into pieces. Enjoy!

Nutrition: calories 248, fat 20.2, fiber 1.4, carbs 4.1, protein 12.8

Morning Tender Chili

Prep time: 10 minutes
Cooking time: 10 minutes
Servings: 4

Ingredients:

- ½ onion
- 8 oz. ground beef
- 1 teaspoon tomato puree
- 1 tablespoon dried dill
- 1 teaspoon dried oregano
- 1 teaspoon dried cilantro
- 1 teaspoon dried parsley
- 6 oz. Cheddar cheese, shredded
- 1 teaspoon mustard
- 1 tablespoon butter

Directions:

Dice the onion and combine it with the ground beef in the bowl. Sprinkle the mixture with the tomato puree, dried dill, dried oregano, dried cilantro, and dried parsley. After this, add mustard and butter. Mix the mixture up. Preheat the air fryer to 380 F. Put the ground beef mixture in the air fryer basket tray and cook the chili for 9 minutes. Stir it carefully after 6th minutes of cooking. When the chili is cooked – sprinkle it with the shredded cheese and stir carefully. Cook the dish for 1 minute more. Then mix the chili mixture carefully again and transfer to the bowls. Taste it!

Nutrition: calories 315, fat 20.8, fiber 0.7, carbs 2.9, protein 28.4

Chicken Casserole

Prep time: 15 minutes
Cooking time: 18 minutes
Servings: 6

Ingredients:

- 9 oz. ground chicken
- 5 oz. bacon, sliced
- ½ onion
- 1 teaspoon salt
- ½ teaspoon ground black pepper
- 1 teaspoon paprika
- 1 teaspoon turmeric
- 6 oz. Cheddar cheese
- 1 egg
- ½ cup cream
- 1 tablespoon almond flour
- 1 tablespoon butter

Directions:

Take the air fryer basket tray and spread it with the butter. Put the ground chicken in the big bowl and add salt and ground black pepper. Add paprika and turmeric and stir the mixture well with the help of the spoon. After this, shredded Cheddar cheese. Beat the egg in the ground chicken mixture until it is homogenous. Then whisk together the cream and almond flour. Peel the onion and dice it. Place the ground chicken in the bottom of the air fryer tray. Sprinkle the ground chicken with the diced onion and cream mixture. Then make the layer from the shredded cheese and sliced bacon. Preheat the air fryer to 380 F. Cook the chicken casserole for 18 minutes. When the casserole is cooked – let it chill briefly. Then serve the chicken casserole. Enjoy!

Nutrition: calories 396, fat 28.6, fiber 1, carbs 3.8, protein 30.4

Herbed Eggs

Prep time: 10 minutes
Cooking time: 17 minutes
Servings: 2

Ingredients:

- 4 eggs
- 1 teaspoon paprika
- 1 tablespoon cream
- 1 tablespoon chives
- ½ teaspoon salt
- 1 teaspoon dried parsley
- 1 teaspoon oregano

Directions:

Put the eggs in the air fryer basket and cook them for 17 minutes at 320 F. Meanwhile, combine the cream, salt, dried parsley, and oregano in the shallow bowl. Chop the chives and add to the cream mixture. When the eggs are cooked – place them in the cold water and let them chill. After this, peel the eggs and cut them into the halves. Remove the egg yolks and add them to the cream mixture. Mash it well with the help of the fork. Then fill the egg whites with the cream-egg yolk mixture. Serve the breakfast immediately. Enjoy!

Nutrition: calories 136, fat 9.3, fiber 0.8, carbs 2.1, protein 11.4

Crunchy Canadian Bacon

Prep time: 7 minutes
Cooking time: 10 minutes
Servings: 4

Ingredients:

- ½ teaspoon ground thyme
- ½ teaspoon ground coriander
- ¼ teaspoon ground black pepper
- ½ teaspoon salt
- 1 teaspoon cream
- 10 oz. Canadian bacon

Directions:

Slice Canadian bacon. Combine the ground thyme, ground coriander, ground black pepper, and salt in the shallow bowl. Shake it gently. Then sprinkle the sliced bacon with the spices from each side. Preheat the air fryer to 360 F. Put the prepared sliced bacon in the air fryer and cook it for 5 minutes. After this, turn the sliced bacon to another side and cook it for 5 minutes more. When the bacon is cooked and get a little bit crunchy – remove the bacon from the air fryer and sprinkle it with the cream gently. Serve it immediately!

Nutrition: calories 150, fat 6.7, fiber 0.1, carbs 1.9, protein 19.6

Kale Fritters

Prep time: 10 minutes
Cooking time: 8 minutes
Servings: 8

Ingredients:

- 12 oz. kale
- ½ onion
- 1 tablespoon butter
- 1 egg
- 2 tablespoons almond flour
- ½ teaspoon salt
- 1 teaspoon paprika
- 1 tablespoon cream
- 1 teaspoon oil

Directions:

Wash the kale carefully and chop it roughly. The place the chopped kale in the blender and blend it until smooth. After this, dice the onion. Beat the egg in the bowl and whisk it using the hand whisker. Add almond flour, salt, paprika, and cream. Stir it. Then add the diced onion and blended kale. Mix it up until you get homogenous fritter dough. Preheat the air fryer to 360 F. Spray the air fryer basket tray with the olive oil inside. Then make the medium fritters from the prepared dough and place them in the air fryer basket tray. Cook the kale fritters for 4 minutes from each side. When the kale fritters are cooked – transfer them from the air fryer and chill. Enjoy!

Nutrition: calories 86, fat 5.6, fiber 1.6, carbs 6.8, protein 3.6

Keto Air Bread

Prep time: 20 minutes
Cooking time: 25 minutes
Servings: 19

Ingredients
- 1 cup almond flour
- 3 eggs
- ¼ cup butter
- 1 teaspoon baking powder
- ¼ teaspoon salt

Directions:
Crack the eggs into the bowl and mix them up using the hand mixer. Then melt the butter until the room temperature. Add the butter to the egg mixture. After this, add salt, baking powder, and almond flour. Knead the smooth non-sticky dough. Cover the prepared dough with the towel and leave for 10 minutes to rest. Meanwhile, preheat the air fryer to 360 F. Place the prepared dough in the air fryer tin and cook the bread for 10 minutes. Then reduce the temperature to 350 F and cook the bread for 15 minutes more. When the time is over – check if the bread is cooked with the help of the toothpick. Transfer the bread to the wooden board and let it chill. Then slice the bread and serve. Taste it!

Nutrition: calories 40, fat 3.9, fiber 0.2, carbs 0.5, protein 1.2

Tuna Boards

Prep time: 10 minutes
Cooking time: 10 minutes
Servings: 4

Ingredients
- 6 oz. bacon, sliced
- ¼ teaspoon salt
- ¼ teaspoon turmeric
- ½ teaspoon ground black pepper
- 6 oz. tuna
- 1 teaspoon cream
- 4 oz. Parmesan
- 1 teaspoon butter

Directions:
Take the air fryer ramekins and place the sliced bacon there. Put the small amount of the butter in every ramekin. Combine the salt, turmeric, and ground black pepper together. Mix it up. Then shred Parmesan. Chop the tuna and combine it with the spice mixture. Place the chopped tuna in the bacon ramekins. Add the cream and shredded cheese. Preheat the air fryer to 360 F. Put the tuna boards in the air fryer basket and cook the dish for 10 minutes. When the tuna boards are cooked – they will have little bit crunchy taste and light brown color. Serve the dish only hot. Enjoy!

Nutrition: calories 411, fat 28.3, fiber 0.1, carbs 1.9, protein 36.2

Breakfast Cookies

Prep time: 10 minutes
Cooking time: 15 minutes
Servings: 6

Ingredients

- ½ cup coconut flour
- ½ cup almond flour
- 1/3 teaspoon salt
- 1 teaspoon baking powder
- 1 teaspoon apple cider vinegar
- 4 oz. bacon, cooked, chopped
- 3 tablespoon butter
- 1 tablespoon cream
- 1 egg

Directions:

Beat the egg in the bowl and whisk it. Add the baking powder, apple cider vinegar, and cream. Stir it gently and add butter. After this, add salt, almond flour, and coconut flour. Sprinkle the mixture with the chopped bacon and knead the smooth, soft, and little bit sticky dough. Preheat the air fryer to 360 F. Cover the air fryer tray with the foil. Make 6 medium balls from the prepared dough and place the balls in the air fryer basket. Cook the cookies for 15 minutes. When the cookies are cooked – let them cool briefly. Then transfer the cooked cookies on the serving plate. Enjoy!

Nutrition: calories 219, fat 16.7, fiber 4.3, carbs 8, protein 9.8

Chicken Hash

Prep time: 10 minutes
Cooking time: 14 minutes
Servings: 3

Ingredients

- 6 oz. cauliflower
- 7 oz. chicken fillet
- 1 tablespoon cream
- 3 tablespoon butter
- 1 teaspoon ground black pepper
- ½ onion
- 1 green pepper
- 1 tablespoon water

Directions:

Chop the cauliflower roughly and put it in the blender. Blend it carefully until you get the cauliflower rice. Chop the chicken fillet into the small pieces. Sprinkle the chicken fillet with the ground black pepper and stir it. Preheat the air fryer to 380 F. Put the prepared chicken in the air fryer basket tray, add water, and cream and cook it for 6 minutes. Then reduce the heat of the air fryer to 360 F. Dice the onion and chop the green pepper. Add the cauliflower rice, diced onion, and chopped green pepper. Add the butter and mix the mixture up. Cook the dish for 8 minutes more. The mix the chicken hash carefully and check if all the ingredients are cooked. Serve the chicken hash immediately. Enjoy!

Nutrition: calories 261, fat 16.8, fiber 2.7, carbs 7.1, protein 21

Chicken Strips

Prep time: 10 minutes
Cooking time: 12 minutes
Servings: 4

Ingredients

- 1 teaspoon paprika
- ½ teaspoon ground black pepper
- 1 tablespoon butter
- ½ teaspoon salt
- 1-pound chicken fillet
- 1 tablespoon cream

Directions:

Cut the chicken fillet into the strips. Sprinkle the chicken strips with the ground black pepper and salt. Then preheat the air fryer to 365 F. Put the butter in the air fryer basket tray and add the chicken strips. Cook the chicken strips for 6 minutes. Then turn the chicken strips to another side and cook them for 5 minutes more. After this, sprinkle the chicken strips with the cream and let them rest for 1 minute. Transfer the cooked chicken strips in the serving plates. Enjoy!

Nutrition: calories 245, fat 11.5, fiber 0.3, carbs 0.6, protein 33

Eggs in Zucchini Nests

Prep time: 10 minutes
Cooking time: 7 minutes
Servings: 4

Ingredients

- 8 oz. zucchini
- 4 eggs
- 4 oz. Cheddar cheese, shredded
- ¼ teaspoon salt
- ½ teaspoon ground black pepper
- ½ teaspoon paprika
- 4 teaspoon butter

Directions:

Grate the zucchini. Place the butter in the ramekins. Add the grated zucchini to make the shape of the nests. After this sprinkle, the zucchini nests with the salt, ground black pepper, and paprika. Beat the eggs in the zucchini nests and sprinkle the eggs with the shredded cheese. Preheat the air fryer to 360 F. Put the ramekins in the air fryer basket and cook the dish for 7 minutes. When the zucchini nests are cooked – let them chill for 2-3 minutes. Serve the zucchini nests in the ramekins. Enjoy!

Nutrition: calories 221, fat 17.7, fiber 0.8, carbs 2.9, protein 13.4

Main Dishes

Pandan Chicken

Prep time: 20 minutes
Cooking time: 10 minutes
Servings: 4

Ingredients

- 15 oz. chicken
- 1 pandan leaf
- ½ onion, diced
- 1 teaspoon minced garlic
- 1 teaspoon chili flakes
- 1 teaspoon stevia
- 1 teaspoon ground black pepper
- 1 teaspoon turmeric
- 1 tablespoon butter
- ¼ cup coconut milk
- 1 tablespoon chives

Directions:

Cut the chicken into 4 big cubes. Put the chicken cubes in the big bowl. Sprinkle the chicken with the minced garlic, diced onion, chili flakes, stevia, ground black pepper, chives, and turmeric. Mix the meat up with the help of the hands. Then cut the pandan leaf into 4 parts. Wrap the chicken cubes into pandan leaf. Pour the coconut milk into the bowl with the wrapped chicken and leave it for 10 minutes. Then preheat the air fryer to 380 F. Put the pandan chicken in the air fryer basket and cook the dish for 10 minutes. When the chicken is cooked – transfer it to the serving plates and let it chill for at least 2-3 minutes. Serve the dish!

Nutrition: calories 250, fat 12.6, fiber 0.9, carbs 3.1, protein 29.9

Bacon Chicken Breast

Prep time: 15 minutes
Cooking time: 16 minutes
Servings: 4

Ingredients

- 1-pound chicken breast, skinless, boneless
- 4 oz. bacon, sliced
- 1 teaspoon paprika
- ¼ cup almond milk
- 1 teaspoon salt
- ½ teaspoon ground black pepper
- 1 teaspoon turmeric
- 1 tablespoon fresh lemon juice
- 2 tablespoon butter
- 1 teaspoon canola oil

Directions:

Beat the chicken breast lightly. Then rub the chicken breast with the paprika, salt, ground black pepper, and turmeric. Sprinkle the chicken breast with the fresh lemon juice. Then place the butter in the center of the chicken breast and roll it. Wrap the chicken roll in the sliced bacon and sprinkle the bacon chicken with the almond milk and canola oil. Preheat the air fryer to 380 F. Put the bacon chicken in the air fryer basket and cook it for 8 minutes. After this, turn the chicken breast to another side and cook it for 8 minutes more. Do not worry if the bacon will be very crunchy – it will give the juicy texture of the chicken breast. When the time is over and the bacon chicken breast is cooked – transfer it to the serving plate and slice. Enjoy!

Nutrition: calories 383, fat 25.4, fiber 0.7, carbs 2.2, protein 35.1

Cheese Chicken Drumsticks

Prep time: 18 minutes
Cooking time: 13 minutes
Servings: 4

Ingredients

- 1-pound chicken drumstick
- 6 oz. Cheddar cheese, sliced
- 1 teaspoon dried rosemary
- 1 teaspoon dried oregano
- ½ teaspoon salt
- ½ teaspoon chili flakes

Directions:

Sprinkle the chicken drumsticks with the dried rosemary, dried oregano, salt, and chili flakes. Massage the chicken drumsticks carefully and leave for 5 minutes to marinate. Preheat the air fryer to 370 F. Place the marinated chicken drumsticks in the air fryer tray and cook them for 10 minutes. After this, turn the chicken drumsticks into another side and cover them with the layer of the sliced cheese. Cook the chicken for 3 minutes more at the same temperature. Then transfer the chicken drumsticks into the big serving plate. Serve the dish only hot – the cheese should be melted. Enjoy!

Nutrition: calories 226, fat 9.8, fiber 0.3, carbs 1, protein 16.4

Succulent Beef Steak

Prep time: 15 minutes
Cooking time: 12 minutes
Servings: 4

Ingredients

- 1 tablespoon butter
- 2 tablespoons fresh orange juice
- 1 teaspoon lime zest
- 1-pound beef steak
- 1 teaspoon ground ginger
- 1 teaspoon dried oregano
- 1 tablespoon cream
- ½ teaspoon minced garlic

Directions:

Combine the fresh orange juice, butter, lime zest, ground ginger, dried oregano, cream, and minced garlic together. Churn the mixture well. Then beat the steak gently. Brush the beefsteak with the churned orange juice carefully and leave the steak for 7 minutes to marinate. After this, preheat the air fryer to 360 F. Put the marinated beefsteak in the air fryer basket and cook the meat for 12 minutes. The meat should have the well-done cooked structure. When the time is over – transfer the cooked meat to the serving plates. Enjoy!

Nutrition: calories 245, fat 10.2, fiber 0.3, carbs 1.7, protein 34.6

Garlic Chicken

Prep time: 20 minutes
Cooking time: 16 minutes
Servings: 4

Ingredients
- 3 oz. fresh coriander root
- 1 teaspoon olive oil
- 3 tablespoon minced garlic
- ¼ lemon, sliced
- ½ teaspoon salt
- 1 teaspoon ground black pepper
- ½ teaspoon chili flakes
- 1 tablespoon dried parsley
- 1-pound chicken tights

Directions:
Peel the fresh coriander and grate it. Then combine the olive oil with the minced garlic, salt, ground black pepper, chili flakes, and dried parsley. Churn the mixture and sprinkle the chicken tights. After this, add the sliced lemon and grated coriander root. Mix the chicken tights carefully and leave them to marinate for 10 minutes in the fridge. Meanwhile, preheat the air fryer to 365 F. Put the chicken tights in the air fryer basket tray. Add all the remaining liquid from the chicken tights and cook the meat for 15 minutes. When the time is over – turn the chicken gently into another side and cook it for 1 minute more. Serve the chicken tights hot. Enjoy!

Nutrition: calories 187, fat 11.4, fiber 1, carbs 3.6, protein 20

Crunchy Chicken Skin

Prep time: 10 minutes
Cooking time: 6 minutes
Servings: 6

Ingredients
- 1-pound chicken skin
- 1 teaspoon dried dill
- ½ teaspoon ground black pepper
- ½ teaspoon chili flakes
- ½ teaspoon salt
- 1 teaspoon butter

Directions:
Slice the chicken skin roughly and sprinkle it with the dried dill, ground black pepper, chili flakes, and salt. Mix the chicken skin up. Melt the butter and add it to the chicken skin mixture. Mix the chicken skin with the help of the spoon. Then preheat the air fryer to 360 F. Put the prepared chicken skin in the air fryer basket. Cook the chicken skin for 3 minutes from each side. Cook the chicken skin more if you want the crunchy effect. Transfer the cooked chicken skin in the paper towel and let it dry. Then serve the chicken skin. Enjoy!

Nutrition: calories 350, fat 31.4, fiber 0.1, carbs 0.2, protein 15.5

Air Frier Pork Ribs

Prep time: 30 minutes
Cooking time: 30 minutes
Servings: 5

Ingredients
- 1 tablespoon apple cider vinegar
- 1 teaspoon cayenne pepper
- 1 teaspoon minced garlic
- 1 teaspoon mustard
- 1 teaspoon chili flakes
- 16 oz. pork ribs
- 1 teaspoon sesame oil
- 1 teaspoon salt
- 1 tablespoon paprika

Directions:
Chop the pork ribs roughly. Then sprinkle the pork ribs with the cayenne pepper, apple cider vinegar, minced garlic, mustard, and chili flakes. Then add the sesame oil and salt. Add paprika and mix the pork ribs carefully. Leave the pork ribs in the fridge for 20 minutes. After this, preheat the air fryer to 360 F. Transfer the pork ribs in the air fryer basket and cook them for 15 minutes. After this, turn the pork ribs to another side and cook the meat for 15 minutes more. Then transfer the pork ribs in the serving bowls. Enjoy!

Nutrition: calories 265, fat 17.4, fiber 0.7, carbs 1.4, protein 24.5

Air Fryer Beef Tongue

Prep time: 10 minutes
Cooking time: 20 minutes
Servings: 6

Ingredients
- 1-pound beef tongue
- 1 teaspoon salt
- 1 teaspoon ground black pepper
- 1 teaspoon paprika
- 1 tablespoon butter
- 4 cup water

Directions:
Preheat the air fryer to 365 F. Put the beef tongue in the air fryer basket tray and add water. Sprinkle the mixture with the salt, ground black pepper, and paprika. Cook the beef tongue for 15 minutes. After this, strain the water from the beef tongue. Cut the beef tongue into the strips. Then toss the butter in the air fryer basket tray and add the beef strips. Cook the beef tongue strips for 5 minutes at 360 F. When the beef tongue is cooked – transfer the dish to the serving plate. Enjoy!

Nutrition: calories 234, fat 18.8, fiber 0.2, carbs 0.4, protein 14.7

Pork Rinds

Prep time: 10 minutes
Cooking time: 7 minutes
Servings: 8

Ingredients

- 1-pound pork rinds
- 1 teaspoon olive oil
- ½ teaspoon salt
- 1 teaspoon chili flakes
- ½ teaspoon ground black pepper

Directions:

Preheat the air fryer to 365 F. Spray the air fryer basket tray with the olive oil inside. Then put the pork rinds in the air fryer basket tray. Sprinkle the pork rinds with the salt, chili flakes, and ground black pepper. Mix them up gently. After this, cook the pork rinds for 7 minutes. When the time is over – shake the pork rinds gently. Transfer the dish to the big serving plate and let it chill for 1-2 minutes. Serve and taste!

Nutrition: calories 329, fat 20.8, fiber 0, carbs 0.1, protein 36.5

Keto Salmon Pie

Prep time: 20 minutes
Cooking time: 30 minutes
Servings: 8

Ingredients

- ½ cup cream
- 1 ½ cup almond flour
- ½ teaspoon baking soda
- 1 tablespoon apple cider vinegar
- 1 onion, diced
- 1-pound salmon
- 1 tablespoon chives
- 1 teaspoon dried oregano
- 1 teaspoon dried dill
- 1 teaspoon butter
- 1 egg
- 1 teaspoon dried parsley
- 1 teaspoon ground paprika

Directions:

Beat the egg in the bowl and whisk it. Then add the cream and keep whisking it for 2 minutes more. After this, add baking soda and apple cider vinegar. Add almond flour and knead the smooth and non-sticky dough. Then chop the salmon into tiny pieces. Sprinkle the chopped salmon with the diced onion, chives, dried oregano, dried dill, dried parsley, and ground paprika. Mix the fish up. Then cut the dough into 2 parts. Cover the air fryer basket tray with the parchment. Put the first part of the dough in the air fryer basket tray and make the crust from it with the help of the fingertips. Then place the salmon filling. Roll the second part of the dough with the help of the rolling pin and cover the salmon filling. Secure the pie edges. Preheat the air fryer to 360 F. Put the air fryer basket tray in the air fryer and cook the pie for 15 minutes. After this, reduce the power to 355 F and cook the pie for 15 minutes more. When the pie is cooked – remove it from the air fryer basket and chill little. Slice the pie and serve. Enjoy!

Nutrition: calories 134, fat 8.1, fiber 1.1, carbs 3.3, protein 13.2

Corn Beef

Prep time: 10 minutes
Cooking time: 19 minutes
Servings: 3

Ingredients:

- 1 onion
- 1 teaspoon black pepper
- ¼ teaspoon cayenne pepper
- 1 cup water
- 1-pound minced beef
- 1 teaspoon butter
- ½ teaspoon ground paprika

Directions:

Peel the onion and slice it finely. Then pour water in the pizza tray and put the sliced onion there. Sprinkle the onion with the black pepper, cayenne pepper, and ground paprika. Then add water and mix the onion up carefully. Preheat the air fryer to 400 F and put the tray with the sliced onion in the air fryer basket. Cook the onion for 4 minutes. After this, remove the tray from the air fryer and add the minced garlic. Mix the onion-meat mixture carefully and return it back in the air fryer. Cook the beef mixture for 7 minutes at the same temperature. After this, mix the meat mixture carefully with the help of the fork and cook the ground beef mixture for 8 minutes more. Then remove the cooked beef from the air fryer and mix it up gently with the help of the fork again. Transfer the cooked beef to the serving plates. Enjoy!

Nutrition: calories 310, fat 10.8, fiber 1.2, carbs 4.2, protein 46.4

Keto Beef Stew

Prep time: 15 minutes
Cooking time: 23 minutes
Servings: 6

Ingredients

- 10 oz. beef short ribs
- 1 cup chicken stock
- 1 garlic clove
- ½ onion
- 4 oz. green peas
- ¼ teaspoon salt
- 1 teaspoon turmeric
- 1 green pepper
- 2 teaspoon butter
- ½ teaspoon chili flakes
- 4 oz. kale

Directions:

Preheat the air fryer to 360 F. Place the butter in the air fryer basket tray. Add the beef short ribs. Sprinkle the beef short ribs with the salt, turmeric, and chili flakes. Cook the beef short ribs for 15 minutes. Meanwhile, remove the seeds from the green pepper and chop it. Chop the kale and dice the onion. When the time is over – pour the chicken stock in the beef short ribs. Add the chopped green pepper and diced onion. After this, sprinkle the mixture with the green peas. Peel the garlic clove and add it to the mixture too. Mix it up using the wooden spatula. Then chop the kale and add it to the stew mixture. Stir the stew mixture one more time and cook it at 360 F for 8 minutes more. When the stew is cooked – let it rest little. Then mix the stew up and transfer to the serving plates. Enjoy!

Nutrition: calories 144, fat 5.8, fiber 1.9, carbs 7, protein 15.7

Chicken Curry

Prep time: 10 minutes
Cooking time: 15 minutes
Servings: 4

Ingredients
- 1 teaspoon olive oil
- 1-pound chicken breast, skinless, boneless
- 1 onion
- 2 teaspoon minced garlic
- 1 tablespoon apple cider vinegar
- 1 tablespoon lemongrass
- ½ cup coconut milk
- ½ cup chicken stock
- 2 tablespoon curry paste

Directions:
Cut the chicken breast into the cubes, Peel the onion and dice it. Then combine the chicken cubes and diced onion together in the air fryer basket tray. Preheat the air fryer to 365 F. Put the chicken mixture in the air fryer and cook it for 5 minutes. After this, add the minced garlic, apple cider vinegar, lemongrass, coconut milk, chicken stock, and curry paste. Mix the mixture up with the help of the wooden spatula. Cook the chicken curry for 10 minutes more at the same temperature. When the time is over and the chicken curry is cooked – remove it from the air fryer and stir one more time. Transfer the dish to the serving plates. Enjoy!

Nutrition: calories 275, fat 15.7, fiber 1.3, carbs 7.2, protein 25.6

Herbed Shredded Beef

Prep time: 15 minutes
Cooking time: 22 minutes
Servings: 8

Ingredients
- 1 teaspoon thyme
- 1 teaspoon ground black pepper
- 1 teaspoon salt
- 1 teaspoon dried dill
- 1 teaspoon mustard
- 4 cup chicken stock
- 2-pound beef steak
- 1 garlic clove, peeled
- 3 tablespoon butter
- 1 bay leaf

Directions:
Preheat the air fryer to 360 F. Meanwhile, combine the thyme, ground black pepper, salt, dried dill, and mustard in the small mixing bowl. After this, sprinkle the beefsteak with the spice mixture from the both sides. Massage the beefsteak with the help of the fingertip to make the meat soak the spices. Then pour the chicken stock in the air fryer. Add the prepared beef steak and bay leaf. Cook the beefsteak for 20 minutes. When the time is over – strain the chicken stock and discard the beefsteak from the air fryer. Shred the meat with the help of 2 forks and return it back in the air fryer basket tray. Add butter and cook the meat for 2 minutes at 365 F. After this, mix the shredded meat carefully with the help of the fork. Transfer the dish to the serving bowls. Enjoy!

Nutrition: calories 265, fat 14, fiber 0.2, carbs 1.2, protein 32.4

Beef Strips with Zucchini Spirals

Prep time: 15 minutes
Cooking time: 13 minutes
Servings: 8

Ingredients

- 1-pound beef brisket
- 1 teaspoon ground black pepper
- 1 tomato
- 1 teaspoon salt
- 1 zucchini
- 1 teaspoon olive oil
- 1 teaspoon Italian spices
- 4 tablespoon water

Directions:

Cut the beef brisket into the strips. Sprinkle the beef strips with the ground black pepper and salt. After this, chop the tomato roughly and transfer it to the blender. Blend it well until you get the smooth puree. After this, spray the air fryer basket tray with the olive oil inside and put the beef strips there. Cook the beef strips for 9 minutes at 365 F. Stir the beef strips carefully after 4 minutes of cooking. Meanwhile, wash the zucchini carefully and make the spirals from the vegetable with the help of the spiralizer. When the time of the cooking of the meat is finished – add the zucchini spirals over the meat. Then sprinkle it with the tomato puree, water, and Italian spices. Cook the dish for 4 minutes more at 360 F. When the time is over and the dish is cooked – stir it gently with the help of the wooden spatula. Serve the dish immediately. Enjoy!

Nutrition: calories 226, fat 5.3, fiber 8, carbs 35.25, protein 12

Delightful Ground Beef Mash

Prep time: 10 minutes
Cooking time: 15 minutes
Servings: 4

Ingredients

- 1-pound ground beef
- 1 white onion
- 1 teaspoon garlic, sliced
- 1 teaspoon ground white pepper
- ¼ cup cream
- 1 teaspoon olive oil
- 2 green peppers
- 1 teaspoon dried dill
- 1 teaspoon cayenne pepper
- 2 teaspoon chicken stock

Directions:

Peel the onion and grate it. Combine the grated onion with the sliced garlic. Mix the mixture carefully with the help of the teaspoon. Then sprinkle the ground beef with the ground white pepper. Add dried dill and cayenne pepper. Spray the air fryer basket tray with the olive oil. Preheat the air fryer to 365 F. Put the spiced ground beef in the air fryer basket tray. Cook the beef mixture for 3 minutes. Then stir it carefully. Add the grated onion mixture and chicken stock. Mix it up gently and cook at the same temperature regime for 2 minutes more. Meanwhile, chop the green peppers into the small pieces. When the time is over – add the chopped green peppers in the air fryer too. Add the cream and stir it till homogenous. Cook the ground beef mixture for 10 minutes more. When the time is over – mash the ground beef mixture with the help of the hand blender. Then transfer it I the serving plates. Serve the dish only hot!

Nutrition: calories 258, fat 9.3, fiber 1.9, carbs 6.8, protein 35.5

Liver Burgers

Prep time: 15 minutes
Cooking time: 10 minutes
Servings: 7

Ingredients

- ½ teaspoon turmeric
- ½ teaspoon ground coriander
- 1 teaspoon ground thyme
- ½ teaspoon salt
- 2 teaspoon butter
- 1 tablespoon almond flour
- 1 tablespoon coconut flour
- 1 teaspoon chili flakes
- 1-pound chicken liver
- 1 egg

Directions:

Grin the chicken liver. Put the ground chicken in the mixing bowl. Beat the egg in the separate bowl and whisk it. Add the turmeric, ground coriander, ground thyme, and salt in the whisked egg mixture. Add the whisked egg mixture in the ground liver. After this, add the coconut flour and almond flour. Mix it up with the help of the spoon. You should get the non-sticky liver mixture. Add more almond flour if desired. Preheat the air fryer to 360 F. Then melt the butter and spread the air fryer basket tray with the melted butter. Make the medium liver burgers and put them in the prepared air fryer basket tray. Cook the burgers for 5 minutes on each side. The burger's sides should be a little bit crunchy. When the liver burgers are cooked – let them chill little. Serve the dish!

Nutrition: calories 155, fat 8.1, fiber 0.9, carbs 2.4, protein 17.7

Sesame Salad with Beef Strips

Prep time: 10 minutes
Cooking time: 12 minutes
Servings: 5

Ingredients

- 2 cup lettuce
- 10 oz. beef brisket
- 2 tablespoon sesame oil
- 1 tablespoon sunflower seeds
- 1 cucumber
- 1 teaspoon ground black pepper
- 1 teaspoon paprika
- 1 teaspoon Italian spices
- 2 teaspoon butter
- 1 teaspoon dried dill
- 2 tablespoon coconut milk

Directions:

Cut the beef brisket into the strips. Sprinkle the beef strips with the ground black pepper, paprika, and dried dill. Preheat the air fryer to 365 F. Put the butter in the air fryer basket tray and melt it. Then add the beef strips and cook them for 6 minutes from 2 sides. Meanwhile, tear the lettuce and toss it in the big salad bowl. Crush the sunflower seeds and sprinkle the lettuce. Chop the cucumber into the small cubes and add the vegetable in the salad bowl too. Then combine the sesame oil and Italian spices together. Stir the oil – the dressing for the salad is cooked. Sprinkle the lettuce mixture with the coconut milk and stir it using 2 wooden spatulas. When the meat is cooked – let it chill until the room temperature. Add the beef strips in the salad bowl. Stir it gently and sprinkle the salad with the sesame oil dressing. Serve the dish immediately. Enjoy!

Nutrition: calories 199, fat 12.4, fiber 0.9, carbs 3.9, protein 18.1

Cayenne Pepper Rib Eye Steak

Prep time: 10 minutes
Cooking time: 13 minutes
Servings: 2

Ingredients

- 1-pound rib eye steak
- 1 teaspoon salt
- 1 teaspoon cayenne pepper
- ½ teaspoon chili flakes
- 3 tablespoon cream
- 1 teaspoon olive oil
- 1 teaspoon lemongrass
- 1 tablespoon butter
- 1 teaspoon garlic powder

Directions:

Preheat the air fryer to 360 F. Take the shallow bowl and combine the cayenne pepper, salt, chili flakes, lemongrass, and garlic powder together. Shake the spices gently. Then sprinkle the rib eye steak with the spice mixture. Melt the butter and combine it with cream and olive oil. Churn the mixture. Pour the churned mixture into the air fryer basket tray. Then add the rib eye steak. Cook the steak for 13 minutes. Do not stir the steak during the cooking. When the steak is cooked – transfer it to the paper towel to make it soaks all the excess fat. Serve the steak. You can slice the steak if desired. Enjoy!

Nutrition: calories 708, fat 59, fiber 0.4, carbs 2.3, protein 40.4

Meatballs Casserole

Prep time: 15 minutes
Cooking time: 21 minutes
Servings: 7

Ingredients

- 1 eggplant
- 10 oz. ground chicken
- 8 oz. ground beef
- 1 teaspoon minced garlic
- 1 teaspoon ground white pepper
- 1 tomato
- 1 egg
- 1 tablespoon coconut flour
- 8 oz. Parmesan, shredded
- 2 tablespoon butter
- 1/3 cup cream

Directions:

Combine the ground chicken and ground beef in the big bowl. Add the minced garlic and ground white pepper. Then beat the egg in the bowl with the ground meat mixture and stir it carefully until the mass is homogeneous. Then add the coconut flour and mix it. Make the small meatballs from the ground meat. Preheat the air fryer to 360 F. Then sprinkle the air fryer basket tray with the butter and pour the cream. Peel the eggplant and chop it. Put the meatballs over the cream and sprinkle them with the chopped eggplant. Then slice the tomato and place it over the eggplant. Make the layer of the shredded cheese over the sliced tomato. After this, put the casserole in the air fryer and cook it for 21 minutes. When the time is over – let the casserole chill until the room temperature or less (depends on the level of the melting of the cheese you like). Serve the casserole and taste it!

Nutrition: calories 314, fat 16.8, fiber 3.4, carbs 7.5, protein 33.9

Juicy Pork Chops

Prep time: 10 minutes
Cooking time: 11 minutes
Servings: 3

Ingredients

- 1 teaspoon peppercorns
- 1 teaspoon kosher salt
- 1 teaspoon minced garlic
- ½ teaspoon dried rosemary
- 1 tablespoon butter
- 13 oz. pork chops

Directions:

Rub the pork chops with the dried rosemary, minced garlic, and kosher salt. Then preheat the air fryer to 365 F. Put the butter and peppercorns in the air fryer basket tray. Melt the butter. Then put the prepared pork chops in the melted butter. Cook the pork chops for 6 minutes. Then turn the pork chops into another side. Cook the pork chops for 5 minutes more. When the meat is cooked – dry it gently with the help of the paper towel. Serve the juicy pork chops immediately. Enjoy!

Nutrition: calories 431, fat 34.4, fiber 0.3, carbs 0.9, protein 27.8

Goulash

Prep time: 10 minutes
Cooking time: 17 minutes
Servings: 6

Ingredients

- 1 white onion
- 2 green peppers, chopped
- 1 teaspoon olive oil
- 14 oz. ground chicken
- 2 tomatoes
- ½ cup chicken stock
- 2 garlic cloves, sliced
- 1 teaspoon salt
- 1 teaspoon ground black pepper
- 1 teaspoon mustard

Directions:

Peel the onion and chop it roughly. Then spray the air fryer basket tray with the olive oil inside. Preheat the air fryer to 365 F. Put the chopped onion in the air fryer basket tray. Add the chopped green pepper and cooked the vegetables for 5 minutes. Then add the ground chicken. Chop the tomatoes into the small cubes and add them in the air fryer mixture too. Cook the mixture for 6 minutes more. After this, add the chicken stock, sliced garlic cloves, salt, ground black pepper, and mustard. Mix the mixture up carefully to get the homogeneous texture. Cook the goulash for 6 minutes more. When the time is over – ladle the cooked dish in the bowls. Enjoy!

Nutrition: calories 161, fat 6.1, fiber 1.7, carbs 6, protein 20.3

Amazing Dinner Meatloaf

Prep time: 15 minutes
Cooking time: 25 minutes
Servings: 12

Ingredients
- 3 tablespoons butter
- 10 oz. ground turkey
- 7 oz. ground chicken
- 1 teaspoon dried dill
- ½ teaspoon ground coriander
- 2 tablespoons almond flour
- 1 tablespoon minced garlic
- 3 oz. fresh spinach
- 1 teaspoon salt
- 1 egg
- ½ tablespoon paprika
- 1 teaspoon sesame oil

Directions:
Put the ground turkey and ground chicken in the big bowl. Sprinkle the ground poultry mixture with the dried dill, ground coriander, almond flour, minced garlic, salt, and paprika. Then grind the fresh spinach and add it to the ground poultry mixture. After this beat the egg in the meat mixture and mix it up until you get the smooth texture of the mixture. Spray the air fryer basket tray with the olive oil. Preheat the air fryer to 350 F. Roll the ground meat mixture gently to make the flat layer. Then put the butter in the center of the meat layer. Then make the shape of the meatloaf from the ground meat mixture. Use the fingertips for this step. Place the prepared meatloaf in the air fryer basket tray. Cook the dish for 25 minutes. When the meatloaf is cooked – let it chill well. Then remove the meatloaf from the air fryer basket tray and slice into servings. Enjoy!

Nutrition: calories 142, fat 9.8, fiber 0.8, carbs 1.7, protein 13

Turkey Meatballs with Dried Dill

Prep time: 15 minutes
Cooking time: 11 minutes
Servings: 9

Ingredients
- 1-pound ground turkey
- 1 teaspoon chili flakes
- ¼ cup chicken stock
- 2 tablespoon dried dill
- 1 egg
- 1 teaspoon salt
- 1 teaspoon paprika
- 1 tablespoon coconut flour
- 2 tablespoons heavy cream
- 1 teaspoon canola oil

Directions:
Beat the egg in the bowl and whisk it with the help of the fork. Add the ground turkey and chili flakes. Sprinkle the mixture with the dried dill, salt, paprika, coconut flour, and mix it up. Make the meatballs from the ground turkey mixture. Preheat the air fryer to 360 F. Spray the air fryer basket tray with the canola oil. Then put the meatballs there. Cook the meatballs for 6 minutes – for 3 minutes from each side. After this, sprinkle the meatballs with the heavy cream. Cook the meatballs for 5 minutes more. When the turkey meatballs are cooked – let them chill for 2-3 minutes. Serve and taste!

Nutrition: calories 124, fat 7.9, fiber 0.5, carbs 1.2, protein 14.8

Chicken Poppers

Prep time: 10 minutes
Cooking time: 10 minutes
Servings: 5

Ingredients

- ½ cup coconut flour
- 1 teaspoon chili flakes
- 1 teaspoon ground black pepper
- 1 teaspoon garlic powder
- 11 oz. chicken breast, boneless, skinless
- 1 tablespoon canola oil

Directions:

Cut the chicken breast into medium cubes and put them in the big bowl. Sprinkle the chicken cubes with the chili flakes, ground black pepper, garlic powder, and stir them well with the help of the hand palms. After this, sprinkle the chicken cubes with the almond flour. Shake the bowl with the chicken cubes gently to coat the meat. Preheat the air fryer to 365 F. Sprinkle the air fryer basket tray with the canola oil. Then toss the chicken cubes there. Cook the chicken poppers for 10 minutes. Turn the chicken poppers into another side after 5 minutes of cooking. Let the cooked chicken poppers chill gently and serve them! Enjoy!

Nutrition: calories 147, fat 5.6, fiber 5, carbs 8.7, protein 15

Parmesan Beef Slices

Prep time: 14 minutes
Cooking time: 25 minutes
Servings: 4

Ingredients

- 12 oz. beef brisket
- 1 teaspoon kosher salt
- 7 oz. Parmesan, sliced
- 1 white onion
- 1 teaspoon turmeric
- 1 teaspoon dried oregano
- 2 teaspoon butter

Directions:

Slice the beef brisket into 4 slices. Sprinkle every beef slice with the turmeric and dried oregano. Then spread the air fryer basket tray with the butter. Put the beef slices there. Peel the white onion and slice it. Make the layer of the sliced onion over the beef slices. Then make the layer of Parmesan cheese. Preheat the air fryer to 365 F. Cook the beef slices for 25 minutes. When the time is over and the beef slices are cooked – let the dish chill little to make the cheese little bit solid. Serve and taste it!

Nutrition: calories 348, fat 18, fiber 0.9, carbs 5, protein 42.1

Beef Jerky

Prep time: 25 minutes
Cooking time: 2.5 hours
Servings: 6

Ingredients
- 14 oz. beef flank steak
- 1 teaspoon chili pepper
- 3 tablespoon apple cider vinegar
- 1 teaspoon ground black pepper
- 1 teaspoon onion powder
- 1 teaspoon garlic powder
- ¼ teaspoon liquid smoke

Directions:
Slice the beefsteak into the medium pieces and then beat every sliced beef pieces. Take the bowl and combine the apple cider vinegar, ground black pepper, onion powder, garlic powder, and liquid smoke. Whisk it gently with the help of the fork. Then transfer the beaten beef pieces in the prepared mixture and stir it well. Leave the meat from 10 minutes until 8 hours for marinating. Then put the marinated beef pieces in the air fryer rack. Cook the beef jerky for 2.5 hours at 150 F. When the beef jerky is cooked – transfer it to the serving plate. Enjoy!

Nutrition: calories 129, fat 4.1, fiber 0.2, carbs 1.1, protein 20.2

Stuffed Beef Heart

Prep time: 15 minutes
Cooking time: 20 minutes
Servings: 4

Ingredients
- 1-pound beef heart
- 1 white onion
- ½ cup fresh spinach
- 1 teaspoon salt
- 1 teaspoon ground black pepper
- 3 cups chicken stock
- 1 teaspoon butter

Directions:
Prepare the beef heart for cooking: remove all the fat from it. Then peel the onion and dice it. Chop the fresh spinach. Combine the diced onion, fresh spinach, and butter together. Stir it. After this, make the cut in the beef heart and fill it with the spinach-onion mixture. Preheat the air fryer to 400 F. Pour the chicken stock into the air fryer basket tray. Then sprinkle the prepared stuffed beef heart with the salt and ground black pepper. Put the prepared beef heart in the air fryer and cook it for 20 minutes. When the time is over – remove the cooked heart from the air fryer and slice it. Then sprinkle the air fryer slices with the remaining liquid from the air fryer. Enjoy!

Nutrition: calories 216, fat 6.8, fiber 0.8, carbs 3.8, protein 33.3

Spicy Pulled Pork

Prep time: 15 minutes
Cooking time: 20 minutes
Servings: 4

Ingredients

- 1 tablespoon chili flakes
- 1 teaspoon ground black pepper
- ½ teaspoon paprika
- 1 teaspoon cayenne pepper
- 1/3 cup cream
- 1 teaspoon kosher salt
- 1-pound pork tenderloin
- 1 teaspoon ground thyme
- 4 cup chicken stock
- 1 teaspoon butter

Directions:

Pour the chicken stock into the air fryer basket tray. Add the pork steak and sprinkle the mixture with the chili flakes, ground black pepper, paprika, cayenne pepper, and kosher salt. Preheat the air fryer to 370 F and cook the meat for 20 minutes. After this, strain the liquid and shred the meat with the help of 2 forks. Then add the butter and cream and mix it. Cook the pulled pork for 4 minutes more at 360 F. When the pulled pork is cooked – let it chill briefly. Serve it!

Nutrition: calories 198, fat 6.8, fiber 0.5, carbs 2.3, protein 30.7

Rosemary Whole Chicken

Prep time: 15 minutes
Cooking time: 75 minutes
Servings: 12

Ingredients

- 6-pound whole chicken
- 1 teaspoon kosher salt
- 1 teaspoon ground black pepper
- 1 teaspoon ground paprika
- 1 tablespoon minced garlic
- 3 tablespoon butter
- 1 teaspoon canola oil
- ¼ cup water
- ½ white onion

Directions:

Rub the whole chicken with the kosher salt and ground black pepper inside and outside. Then sprinkle it with the ground paprika and minced garlic. Peel the onion and dice it. Put the diced onion inside the whole chicken. Then add the butter. Rub the chicken with the canola oil outside. Preheat the air fryer to 360 F and pour water in the air fryer basket. Then place the rack and put the whole chicken there. Cook the chicken for 75 minutes. When the chicken is cooked – it will have little bit crunchy skin. Cut the cooked dish into the servings. Serve it and taste! Enjoy!

Nutrition: calories 464, fat 20.1, fiber 0.2, carbs 0.9, protein 65.8

Pork Bites

Prep time: 10 minutes
Cooking time: 14 minutes
Servings: 6

Ingredients
- 1-pound pork tenderloin
- 2 eggs
- 1 teaspoon butter
- ¼ cup almond flour
- 1 teaspoon kosher salt
- 1 teaspoon paprika
- 1 teaspoon ground coriander
- ½ teaspoon lemon zest

Directions:
Chop the pork tenderloin into the big cubes. Then sprinkle the pork cubes with the kosher salt, paprika, ground coriander, and lemon zest. Mix the meat gently. Crack the egg into the bowl and whisk it. Sprinkle the meat cubes with the egg mixture. Coat every pork cube in the almond flour. Preheat the air fryer to 365 F. Put the butter in the air fryer basket tray and then put the pork bites there. Cook the pork bites for 14 minutes. Turn the pork bites into another side after 7 minutes of cooking. When the pork bites are cooked – serve them hot. Enjoy!

Nutrition: calories 142, fat 5.4, fiber 0.3, carbs 0.6, protein 21.9

Keto Turkey Rolls

Prep time: 10 minutes
Cooking time: 12 minutes
Servings: 4

Ingredients
- 1-pound turkey fillet
- 2 tablespoon garlic clove, sliced
- 1 teaspoon apple cider vinegar
- ½ white onion
- ½ teaspoon salt
- 1 teaspoon paprika
- 1 teaspoon dried dill
- 1 tablespoon chives
- 4 teaspoon butter

Directions:
Cut the turkey fillet into 4 parts. Then beat every turkey fillet gently. Sprinkle the turkey fillets with the apple cider vinegar, salt, paprika, and dried dill. Chop the onion and combine it with the sliced garlic clove. Add the chives and butter. Mix the mixture until homogenous. Then place the churned garlic mixture in the center of every turkey fillet. Roll the fillets and secure the rolls with the toothpicks well. Preheat the air fryer to 360 F. Put the turkey rolls in the air fryer basket tray and cook the dish for 12 minutes. Turn the rolls into another side once per cooking. Transfer the cooked juicy turkey rolls on the plate and serve them hot. Enjoy!

Nutrition: calories 155, fat 4.5, fiber 0.6, carbs 3.2, protein 24.2

Chicken Stew

Prep time: 15 minutes
Cooking time: 12 minutes
Servings: 6

Ingredients

- 8 oz. chicken breast
- 1 white onion
- ½ cup spinach
- 2 cups chicken stock
- 5 oz. white cabbage
- 6 oz. cauliflower
- 1/3 cup heavy cream
- 1 teaspoon salt
- 1 green pepper
- 1 teaspoon paprika
- 1 teaspoon cayenne pepper
- 1 teaspoon butter
- 1 teaspoon ground cilantro

Directions:

Cut the chicken breast into the big cubes. Sprinkle the chicken cubes with the salt, paprika, cayenne pepper, and ground cilantro. Preheat the air fryer to 365 F. Put the butter in the air fryer basket tray and melt it. Then add the chicken cubes and cook them for 4 minutes. Meanwhile, chop the spinach and dice the onion. Then shred the cabbage and cut the cauliflower into the small florets. Then chop the green pepper. When the time is over – add all the prepared ingredients in the air fryer basket tray. Pour the heavy cream and chicken stock. Set the air fryer to 360 F and cook the stew for 8 minutes more. When the stew is cooked – stir it gently with the help of the spatula. Serve the cooked chicken stew immediately. Enjoy!

Nutrition: calories 102, fat 4.5, fiber 2.3, carbs 6.4, protein 9.8

Keto-Friendly Chicken Pizza

Prep time: 15 minutes
Cooking time: 12 minutes
Servings: 6

Ingredients

- 10 oz. ground chicken
- 1 teaspoon minced garlic
- 1 teaspoon almond flour
- ½ teaspoon salt
- 1 teaspoon ground black pepper
- 1 large egg
- 6 oz. Cheddar cheese, shredded
- ½ teaspoon dried dill

Directions:

Put the ground chicken in the bowl. Sprinkle it with the minced garlic, almond flour, salt, ground black pepper, and dried dill. Then crack the egg in the ground chicken mixture and mix it up with the help of the spoon. When you get the homogenous and smooth texture of the ground chicken – the mixture is done. Preheat the air fryer to 380 F. Cover the air fryer pizza tray with the parchment. Then place the ground chicken mixture in the air fryer pizza tray and make the shape of the pizza crust. Cook the chicken pizza crust for 8 minutes. Then remove the chicken pizza crust from the air fryer and sprinkle it with the shredded cheese generously. Cook the pizza for 4 minutes more at 365 F. When the pizza is cooked – let it chill little. Slice the pizza into the servings. Enjoy!

Nutrition: calories 244, fat 16.1, fiber 0.6, carbs 1.9, protein 22.9

Pork Meatballs Stuffed with Cheddar Cheese

Prep time: 15 minutes
Cooking time: 8 minutes
Servings: 6

Ingredients

- 1-pound ground pork
- 5 oz. Cheddar cheese
- 1 tablespoon dried oregano
- 1 large egg
- ½ teaspoon salt
- 1 teaspoon paprika
- 1 tablespoon butter
- ½ teaspoon nutmeg
- 1 teaspoon minced garlic
- ½ teaspoon ground ginger

Directions:

Crack the egg into the bowl and whisk it. Then sprinkle the whisked egg with the salt, paprika, nutmeg, and ground ginger. Stir it gently and add the ground pork. After this, add dried oregano and minced garlic. Mix the mixture up using the spoon. When you get the homogenous forcemeat – make 6 medium balls. Cut Cheddar cheese into 6 medium cubes. Fill the pork meatballs with the cheese cubes. Preheat the air fryer to 365 F. Toss the butter in the air fryer basket tray and melt it. Then put the pork meatballs and cook them for 8 minutes. Stir the meatballs once after 4 minutes of cooking. When the pork meatballs are cooked – transfer them to the plates and serve hot. Enjoy!

Nutrition: calories 295, fat 20.6, fiber 0, carbs 3, protein 23

Beef Pieces with Tender Broccoli

Prep time: 10 minutes
Cooking time: 13 minutes
Servings: 4

Ingredients

- 6 oz. broccoli
- 10 oz. beef brisket
- 1 white onion
- 1 teaspoon paprika
- 1/3 cup water
- 1 teaspoon canola oil
- 1 teaspoon butter
- 1 tablespoon flax seeds
- ½ teaspoon chili flakes

Directions:

Cut the beef brisket into the medium/convenient pieces. Sprinkle the beef pieces with the paprika and chili flakes. Mix the meat up with the help of the hands. Then preheat the air fryer to 360 F. Spray the air fryer basket tray with the canola oil. Put the beef pieces in the air fryer basket tray and cook the meat for 7 minutes. Stir it once during the cooking. Meanwhile, separate the broccoli into the florets. When the time is over – add the broccoli florets in the air fryer basket tray. Sprinkle the ingredients with the flax seeds and butter. Add water. Slice the onion and add it in the air fryer basket tray too. Stir it gently using the wooden spatula. Then cook the dish at 265 F for 6 minutes more. When the broccoli is tender – the dish is cooked. Serve the dish little bit chilled. Enjoy!

Nutrition: calories 187, fat 7.3, fiber 2.4, carbs 6.2, protein 23.4

Chicken Lasagna with Eggplants

Prep time: 21 minutes
Cooking time: 17 minutes
Servings: 8

Ingredients

- 6 oz Cheddar cheese, shredded
- 7 oz Parmesan cheese, shredded
- 2 eggplants
- 1-pound ground chicken
- 1 teaspoon paprika
- 1 teaspoon salt
- ½ teaspoon cayenne pepper
- ½ cup heavy cream
- 2 teaspoon butter
- 1 white onion, diced

Directions:

Take the air fryer basket tray and spread it with the butter. Then peel the eggplants and slice them. Separate the sliced eggplants into 3 parts. Combine the ground chicken with the paprika, salt, cayenne pepper, and diced onion. Mix the mixture up. Separate the ground chicken mixture into 2 parts. Make the layer of the first part of the sliced eggplant in the air fryer basket tray. Then make the layer of the ground chicken mixture. After this, sprinkle the ground chicken layer with the half of the shredded Cheddar cheese, then cover the cheese with the second part of the sliced eggplant. The next step is to make the layer of the ground chicken and all shredded Cheddar cheese, Cover the cheese layer with the last part of the sliced eggplants. Then sprinkle the eggplants with shredded Parmesan cheese. Pour the heavy cream and add butter. Preheat the air fryer to 365 F. Cook the lasagna for 17 minutes. When the time is over – let the lasagna chill gently. Serve it!

Nutrition: calories 348, fat 20.6, fiber 5.3, carbs 10.9, protein 31.4

Salmon Casserole

Prep time: 20 minutes
Cooking time: 12 minutes
Servings: 8

Ingredients

- 7 oz Cheddar cheese, shredded
- ½ cup cream
- 1-pound salmon fillet
- 1 tablespoon dried dill
- 1 teaspoon dried parsley
- 1 teaspoon salt
- 1 teaspoon ground coriander
- ½ teaspoon ground black pepper
- 2 green pepper, chopped
- 1 white onion, diced
- 7 oz bok choy, chopped
- 1 tablespoon canola oil

Directions:

Sprinkle the salmon fillet with the dried dill, dried parsley, ground coriander, and ground black pepper. Massage the salmon fillet gently and leave it for 5 minutes to make the fish soaks the spices. Meanwhile, sprinkle the air fryer casserole tray with the canola oil inside. After this, cut the salmon fillet into the cubes. Separate the salmon cubes into 2 parts. Then place the first part of the salmon cubes in the casserole tray. Sprinkle the fish with the chopped bok choy, diced onion, and chopped green pepper. After this, place the second part of the salmon cubes over the vegetables. Then sprinkle the casserole with the shredded cheese and heavy cream. Preheat the air fryer to 380 F. Cook the salmon casserole for 12 minutes. When the dish is cooked – it will have a crunchy light brown crust. Serve it and enjoy!

Nutrition: calories 216, fat 14.4, fiber 1.1, carbs 4.3, protein 18.2

Bacon Pork Bites

Prep time: 15 minutes
Cooking time: 14 minutes
Servings: 6

Ingredients

- 1-pound pork brisket
- 6 oz. bacon, sliced
- 1 teaspoon salt
- 1 teaspoon turmeric
- ½ teaspoon red pepper
- 1 teaspoon olive oil
- 1 tablespoon apple cider vinegar

Directions:

Cut the pork brisket into the medium bites. Then put the pork bites in the big mixing bowl. Sprinkle the meat with the turmeric, salt, red pepper, and apple cider vinegar. Mix the pork bites carefully and leave them for 10 minutes to marinate. Then wrap the pork bites in the sliced bacon. Secure the pork bites with the toothpicks. Preheat the air fryer to 370 F. Put the prepared bacon pork bites on the air fryer tray. Cook the pork bites for 8 minutes. After this, turn the pork bites into another side. Cook the dish for 6 minutes more. When the bacon pork bites are cooked – let them in the air fryer for 2 minutes. Then transfer the dish to the serving plate. Enjoy!

Nutrition: calories 239, fat 13.7, fiber 0.2, carbs 2.8, protein 26.8

Sweet Chicken Breast

Prep time: 20 minutes
Cooking time: 12 minutes
Servings: 4

Ingredients

- 1-pound chicken breast, boneless, skinless
- 3 tablespoon Stevia extract
- 1 teaspoon ground white pepper
- ½ teaspoon paprika
- 1 teaspoon cayenne pepper
- 1 teaspoon lemongrass
- 1 teaspoon lemon zest
- 1 tablespoon apple cider vinegar
- 1 tablespoon butter

Directions:

Sprinkle the chicken breast with the apple cider vinegar. After this, rub the chicken breast with the ground white pepper, paprika, cayenne pepper, lemongrass, and lemon zest. Leave the chicken breast for 5 minutes to marinate. After this, rub the chicken breast with the stevia extract and leave it for 5 minutes more. Preheat the air fryer to 380 F. Rub the prepared chicken breast with the butter and place it in the air fryer basket tray. Cook the chicken breast for 12 minutes. Turn the chicken breast into another side after 6 minutes of cooking. Serve the dish hot! Enjoy!

Nutrition: calories 160, fat 5.9, fiber 0.4, carbs 1, protein 24.2

Garlic Lamb Shank

Prep time: 15 minutes
Cooking time: 24 minutes
Servings: 5

Ingredients

- 17 oz. lamb shanks
- 2 tablespoon garlic, peeled
- 1 teaspoon kosher salt
- 1 tablespoon dried parsley
- 1 teaspoon chives
- 1 white onion, chopped
- ½ cup chicken stock
- 1 teaspoon butter
- 1 teaspoon dried rosemary
- 1 teaspoon nutmeg
- ½ teaspoon ground black pepper

Directions:

Chop the garlic roughly. Make the cuts in the lamb shank and fill the cuts with the chopped garlic. Then sprinkle the lamb shank with the kosher salt, dried parsley, dried rosemary, nutmeg, and ground black pepper. Stir the spices on the lamb shank gently. Then put the butter and chicken stock in the air fryer basket tray. Preheat the air fryer to 380 F. Put the chopped onion and chives in the air fryer basket tray. Add the lamb shank and cook the meat for 24 minutes. When the lamb shank is cooked – transfer it to the serving plate and sprinkle with the remaining liquid from the cooked meat. Enjoy!

Nutrition: calories 205, fat 8.2, fiber 0.8, carbs 3.8, protein 27.2

Indian Meatballs with Lamb

Prep time: 10 minutes
Cooking time: 14 minutes
Servings: 8

Ingredients

- 1 garlic clove
- 1 tablespoon butter
- 1 white onion
- ¼ tablespoon turmeric
- 1/3 teaspoon cayenne pepper
- 1 teaspoon ground coriander
- ¼ teaspoon bay leaf
- 1 teaspoon salt
- 1-pound ground lamb
- 1 egg
- 1 teaspoon ground black pepper

Directions:

Peel the garlic clove and mince it. Combine the minced garlic with the ground lamb. Then sprinkle the meat mixture with the turmeric, cayenne pepper, ground coriander, bay leaf, salt, and ground black pepper. Beat the egg in the forcemeat. Then grate the onion and add it in the lamb forcemeat too. Mix it up to make the smooth mass. Then preheat the air fryer to 400 F. Put the butter in the air fryer basket tray and melt it. Then make the meatballs from the lamb mixture and place them in the air fryer basket tray. Cook the dish for 14 minutes. Stir the meatballs twice during the cooking. Serve the cooked meatballs immediately. Enjoy!

Nutrition: calories 134, fat 6.2, fiber 0.4, carbs 1.8, protein 16.9

Korean Beef Bowl

Prep time: 15 minutes
Cooking time: 18 minutes
Servings: 4

Ingredients

- 1 tablespoon minced garlic
- 1 teaspoon ground ginger
- 1 white onion, chopped
- 2 tablespoon apple cider vinegar
- 1 teaspoon stevia extract
- 1 tablespoon flax seeds
- 1 teaspoon olive oil
- 1 teaspoon canola oil
- 1 tablespoon chives
- 1-pound ground beef
- 4 tablespoon chicken stock

Directions:

Sprinkle the ground beef with the apple cider vinegar and stir the meat with the help of the spoon. After this, sprinkle the ground beef with the ground ginger, minced garlic, and olive oil. Mix it up. Preheat the air fryer to 370 F. Put the ground beef in the air fryer basket tray and cook it for 8 minutes. After this, stir the ground beef carefully and sprinkle with the chopped onion, flax seeds, canola oil, chives, and chicken stock. Mix the dish up and cook it for 10 minutes more. When the time is over – stir the dish carefully. Serve Korean beef bowl immediately. Enjoy!

Nutrition: calories 258, fat 10.1, fiber 1.2, carbs 4.2, protein 35.3

Keto Lamb Kleftiko

Prep time: 25 minutes
Cooking time: 30 minutes
Servings: 6

Ingredients

- 2 oz. garlic clove, peeled
- 1 tablespoon dried oregano
- ½ lemon
- ¼ tablespoon ground cinnamon
- 3 tablespoon butter, frozen
- 18 oz. leg of lamb
- 1 cup heavy cream
- 1 teaspoon bay leaf
- 1 teaspoon dried mint
- 1 tablespoon canola oil

Directions:

Crush the garlic cloves and combine them with the dried oregano, and ground cinnamon. Mix it. Then chop the lemon. Sprinkle the leg of lamb with the crushed garlic mixture. Then rub it with the chopped lemon. Combine the heavy cream, bay leaf, and dried mint together. Whisk the mixture well. After this, add the canola oil and whisk it one more time more. Then pour the cream mixture on the leg of lamb and stir it carefully. Leave the leg of lamb for 10 minutes to marinate. Preheat the air fryer to 380 F. Chop the butter and sprinkle the marinated lamb. Then place the leg of lamb in the air fryer basket tray and sprinkle it with the remaining cream mixture. Then sprinkle the meat with the chopped butter. Cook the meat for 30 minutes. When the time is over – remove the meat from the air fryer and sprinkle it gently with the remaining cream mixture. Serve it!

Nutrition: calories 318, fat 21.9, fiber 0.9, carbs 4.9, protein 25.1

Pork Chops with Keto Gravy

Prep time: 15 minutes
Cooking time: 17 minutes
Servings: 4

Ingredients

- 1-pound pork chops
- 1 teaspoon kosher salt
- ½ teaspoon ground cinnamon
- 1 teaspoon ground white pepper
- 1 cup heavy cream
- 6 oz. white mushrooms
- 1 tablespoon butter
- ½ teaspoon ground ginger
- 1 teaspoon ground turmeric
- 1 white onion, chopped
- 1 garlic clove, chopped

Directions:

Sprinkle the pork chops with the kosher salt, ground cinnamon, ground white pepper, and ground turmeric. Preheat the air fryer to 375 F. Pour the heavy cream in the air fryer basket tray. Then slice the white mushrooms and add them in the heavy cream. After this, add butter, ground ginger, chopped onion, and chopped garlic. Cook the gravy for 5 minutes. Then stir the cream gravy and add the pork chops. Cook the pork chops at 400 F for 12 minutes. When the time is over stir the pork chops gently and transfer them to the serving plates. Enjoy!

Nutrition: calories 518, fat 42.4, fiber 1.5, carbs 6.2, protein 28

Fragrant Pork Tenderloin

Prep time: 20 minutes
Cooking time: 15 minutes
Servings: 3

Ingredients:

- ½ teaspoon saffron
- 1 teaspoon sage
- ½ teaspoon ground cinnamon
- 1 teaspoon garlic powder
- 1 teaspoon onion powder
- 1-pound pork tenderloin
- 3 tablespoon butter
- 1 garlic clove, crushed
- 1 tablespoon apple cider vinegar

Directions:

Combine the saffron, sage, ground cinnamon, garlic powder, and onion powder together in the shallow bowl. Then shake the spices gently to make them homogenous. After this, coat the pork tenderloin in the spice mixture. Rub the pork tenderloin with the crushed garlic and sprinkle the meat with the apple cider vinegar. Leave the pork tenderloin for 10 minutes to marinate. Meanwhile, preheat the air fryer to 320 F. Put the pork tenderloin in the air fryer tray and place the butter over the meat. Cook the meat for 15 minutes. When the meat is cooked – let it chill briefly. Slice the pork tenderloin and serve it. Enjoy!

Nutrition: calories 328, fat 16.9, fiber 0.5, carbs 2.2, protein 40

Lemon Duck Legs

Prep time: 25 minutes
Cooking time: 25 minutes
Servings: 6

Ingredients:

- 1 lemon
- 2-pound duck legs
- 1 teaspoon ground coriander
- 1 teaspoon ground nutmeg
- 1 teaspoon kosher salt
- ½ teaspoon dried rosemary
- 1 tablespoon olive oil
- 1 teaspoon stevia extract
- ¼ teaspoon sage

Directions:

Squeeze the juice from the lemon and grate the zest. Combine the lemon juice and lemon zest together in the big mixing bowl. Add the ground coriander, ground nutmeg, kosher salt, dried rosemary, and sage. Sprinkle the liquid with the olive oil and stevia extract. Whisk it carefully and put the duck legs there. Stir the duck legs and leave them for 15 minutes to marinate. Meanwhile, preheat the air fryer to 380 F. Put the marinated duck legs in the air fryer and cook them for 25 minutes. Turn the duck legs into another side after 15 minutes of cooking. When the duck legs are cooked – let them cool little. Serve and enjoy!

Nutrition: calories 296, fat 11.5, fiber 0.5, carbs 1.6, protein 44.2

Chili Pepper Lamb Chops

Prep time: 20 minutes
Cooking time: 10 minutes
Servings: 6

Ingredients:

- 21 oz. lamb chops
- 1 teaspoon chili pepper
- ½ teaspoon chili flakes
- 1 teaspoon onion powder
- 1 teaspoon garlic powder
- 1 teaspoon cayenne pepper
- 1 tablespoon canola oil
- 1 tablespoon butter
- ½ teaspoon lime zest

Directions:

Melt the butter and combine it with the canola oil. Whisk the liquid and add chili pepper, chili flakes, onion powder, garlic powder, cayenne pepper, and lime zest. Whisk it well. Then sprinkle the lamb chops with the prepared oily marinade. Leave the meat for at least 5 minutes in the fridge. Preheat the air fryer to 400 F. Place the marinated lamb chops in the air fryer and cook them for 5 minutes. After this, open the air fryer and turn the lamb chops into another side. Cook the lamb chops for 5 minutes more. When the meat is cooked – transfer it to the serving plates. Enjoy!

Nutrition: calories 227, fat 11.6, fiber 0.2, carbs 1, protein 28.1

Keto Kebab

Prep time: 15 minutes
Cooking time: 10 minutes
Servings: 5

Ingredients:
- 14 oz. chicken fillet
- ½ cup heavy cream
- 1 teaspoon kosher salt
- ½ teaspoon ground black pepper
- 1 teaspoon turmeric
- 1 teaspoon curry powder
- 1 teaspoon olive oil

Directions:
Combine the heavy cream with the kosher salt, ground black pepper, turmeric, and curry powder. Whisk the mixture well. Add oil and whisk it again. Cut the chicken fillet into pieces. Add the chicken pieces to the prepared heavy cream mixture and stir it carefully. Preheat the air fryer to 360 F. Put the chicken kebab in the air fryer rack and cook it for 10 minutes. When the kababs are cooked – remove the chicken pieces from the air fryer. Enjoy!

Nutrition: calories 204, fat 11.4, fiber 0.3, carbs 1, protein 23.3

Swedish Meatballs

Prep time: 15 minutes
Cooking time: 11 minutes
Servings: 6

Ingredients:
- 1 tablespoon almond flour
- 1-pound ground beef
- 1 teaspoon dried parsley
- 1 teaspoon dried dill
- ½ teaspoon ground nutmeg
- 1 oz. white onion, chopped
- 1 teaspoon garlic powder
- 1 teaspoon salt
- ½ cup heavy cream
- ¼ cup chicken stock
- 1 teaspoon mustard
- 1 teaspoon ground black pepper
- 1 tablespoon butter

Directions:
Combine the ground beef and almond flour together in the bowl. Add the dried dill, dried parsley, ground nutmeg, garlic powder, chopped onion, salt, ground black pepper, and mustard. Mix the mixture up to get the smooth forcemeat. After this, make the meatballs from the beef forcemeat. Preheat the air fryer to 380 F. Put the beef meatballs in the air fryer basket tray. Add the butter and cook the dish for 5 minutes. After this, turn the meatballs into another side. Sprinkle the meatballs with the heavy cream and chicken stock. Cook the meatballs for 6 minutes more. When the meatballs are cooked – serve them immediately with the cream gravy. Enjoy!

Nutrition: calories 227, fat 12.9, fiber 0.9, carbs 2.7, protein 24.6

Side Dishes

Shirataki Noodles

Prep time: 5 minutes
Cooking time: 3 minutes
Servings: 4

Ingredients:

- 2 cups water
- 1 teaspoon salt
- 1 tablespoon Italian seasoning
- 8 oz shirataki noodles

Directions:

Preheat the air fryer to 365 F. Pour the water in the air fryer basket tray and preheat it for 3 minutes. Then add the shirataki noodles, salt, and Italian seasoning. Cook the shirataki noodles for 1 minute at the same temperature. Then strain the noodles and cook them for 2 minutes more at 360 F. When the shirataki noodles are cooked – let them chill for 1-2 minutes. Stir the noodles gently. Serve it!

Nutrition: calories 16, fat 1, fiber 0, carbs 1.4, protein 0

Turmeric Cauliflower Rice

Prep time: 8 minutes
Cooking time: 10 minutes
Servings: 6

Ingredients:

- 1 white onion, diced
- 3 tablespoon butter
- 1 teaspoon salt
- 1-pound cauliflower
- 1 teaspoon turmeric
- 1 teaspoon minced garlic
- 1 teaspoon ground ginger
- 1 cup chicken stock

Directions:

Wash the cauliflower and chop it roughly. Then place the chopped cauliflower in the blender and blend it till you get the rice texture of the cauliflower. Transfer the cauliflower rice to the mixing bowl. Add the diced onion. After this, sprinkle the vegetable mixture with the salt, turmeric, minced garlic, and ground ginger. Mix it up. Preheat the air fryer to 370 F. Put the cauliflower rice mixture there. Add the butter and chicken stock. Cook the cauliflower rice for 10 minutes. When the time is over – remove the cauliflower rice from the air fryer and strain the excess liquid. Stir it gently. Enjoy!

Nutrition: calories 82, fat 6, fiber 2.4, carbs 6.5, protein 2

Taco Salad

Prep time: 10 minutes
Cooking time: 12 minutes
Servings: 8

Ingredients:

- 12 oz. ground beef
- 1 teaspoon salt
- 1 teaspoon paprika
- 1 teaspoon turmeric
- 1 teaspoon chili pepper
- ½ teaspoon chili flakes
- 1 teaspoon ground black pepper
- 8 oz. Cheddar cheese
- 1 tablespoon sesame oil
- 1 tomato
- ¼ cup heavy cream
- 1 cup lettuce

Directions:

Combine the ground beef with the salt, paprika, turmeric, chili pepper, chili flakes, and ground black pepper. Stir the ground meat mixture with the help of the fork. Sprinkle the ground beef mixture with the sesame oil and place it in the air fryer basket tray. Cook the ground beef at 365 F for 12 minutes. Stir it once during the cooking. Meanwhile, chop the tomato roughly and tear the lettuce. Place the vegetables in the big salad bowl. Cut Cheddar cheese into the cubes and add them to the lettuce mixture. When the ground beef is cooked – let it chill till the room temperature. Add the ground beef in the lettuce salad. Sprinkle the dish with the heavy cream and stir it using two wooden spatulas. Serve it!

Nutrition: calories 160, fat 13, fiber 0.4, carbs 1.5, protein 9.5

Spiced Asparagus

Prep time: 9 minutes
Cooking time: 6 minutes
Servings: 6

Ingredients:

- 1-pound asparagus
- 1 teaspoon salt
- 1 teaspoon chili flakes
- ½ teaspoon ground white pepper
- 1 tablespoon sesame oil
- 1 tablespoon flax seeds

Directions:

Combine the sesame oil with the salt, chili flakes, and ground white pepper. Churn the mixture. Preheat the air fryer to 400 F. Place the asparagus in the air fryer basket tray and sprinkle it with the sesame oil-spice mixture. Cook the asparagus for 6 minutes. When the dish is cooked – let it chill for some minutes. Serve it!

Nutrition: calories 42, fat 2.7, fiber 2, carbs 3.4, protein 1.9

Zucchini Gratin

Prep time: 15 minutes
Cooking time: 13 minutes
Servings: 6

Ingredients:
- 2 zucchini
- 1 tablespoon dried parsley
- 1 tablespoon coconut flour
- 5 oz. Parmesan cheese, shredded
- 1 teaspoon butter
- 1 teaspoon ground black pepper

Directions:

Combine the dried parsley, coconut flour, ground black pepper, and shredded cheese in the big bowl together. Shake it gently to make the homogenous mass. Then wash the zucchini and slice them. Then cut the zucchini to make the squares. Spread the air fryer basket tray with the butter and place the zucchini squares there. Preheat the air fryer to 400 F. Sprinkle the zucchini squares with the dried parsley mixture. Cook the zucchini gratin for 13 minutes. When the zucchini gratin is cooked it will have the light brown color of the surface. Serve it!

Nutrition: calories 98, fat 6, fiber 1.3, carbs 4.2, protein 8.6

Winter Squash Spaghetti

Prep time: 10 minutes
Cooking time: 10 minutes
Servings: 8

Ingredients:
- 4 tablespoons heavy cream
- 1 cup chicken stock
- 1-pound winter squash
- 1 teaspoon salt
- 1 teaspoon ground black pepper
- 1 teaspoon butter

Directions:

Peel the winter squash and grate it to get the spaghetti. Preheat the air fryer to 400 F. Put the winter squash spaghetti in the air fryer basket tray. Sprinkle it with the chicken stock and salt. Add the ground black pepper and cook the dish for 10 minutes. When the time is over – strain the excess liquid from the winter squash spaghetti. Then add the butter and heavy cream and stir it. Serve the side dish immediately. Enjoy!

Nutrition: calories 55, fat 3.4, fiber 0.9, carbs 6.4, protein 0.7

Kale Mash

Prep time: 10 minutes
Cooking time: 12 minutes
Servings: 7

Ingredients:

- 1-pound Italian dark leaf kale
- 7 oz. Parmesan, shredded
- 1 teaspoon salt
- 1 cup heavy cream
- 1 teaspoon butter
- 1 teaspoon ground black pepper
- 1 white onion, diced

Directions:

Chop the kale carefully and place it in the air fryer basket tray. Sprinkle the chopped kale with the salt, butter, ground black pepper, diced onion, and heavy cream. Preheat the air fryer to 250 F. Cook the kale for 12 minutes. When the time is over – mix the kale mash carefully to make it homogenous.Serve the kale mash and enjoy!

Nutrition: calories 180, fat 13.2, fiber 1.7, carbs 6.8, protein 10.9

Stewed Celery Stalk

Prep time: 10 minutes
Cooking time: 8 minutes
Servings: 6

Ingredients:

- 1-pound celery stalk
- 1 tablespoon butter
- 1 white onion, sliced
- 1 cup chicken stock
- 2 tablespoons heavy cream
- 1 teaspoon salt
- 1 tablespoon paprika

Directions:

Chop the celery stalk roughly. Pour the chicken stock into the air fryer basket tray and add the sliced onion. Preheat the air fryer to 400 F. Cook the onion for 4 minutes. After this, reduce the heat to 365 F. Add the chopped celery stalk, butter, salt, paprika, and heavy cream. Mix the vegetable mixture. Cook the celery for 8 minutes more. When the time is over – the celery stalk should be very soft. Chill the side dish to the room temperature. Serve it and enjoy!

Nutrition: calories 59, fat 4.2, fiber 2, carbs 4.9, protein 1.1

White Mushrooms with Spicy Cream

Prep time: 10 minutes
Cooking time: 12 minutes
Servings: 4

Ingredients:

- 9 oz. white mushrooms
- 1 teaspoon garlic, sliced
- 1 onion, sliced
- 1 cup cream
- 1 teaspoon butter
- 1 teaspoon olive oil
- 1 teaspoon ground red pepper
- 1 teaspoon chili flakes

Directions:

Slice the white mushrooms. Sprinkle the white mushrooms with the chili flakes and ground red pepper. Mix the mixture up. After this, preheat the air fryer to 400 F. Pour the olive oil in the air fryer basket tray. Then add the sliced mushrooms and cook the vegetables for 5 minutes. After this, add the sliced onion, cream, butter, sliced garlic, and mix the mushroom gently with the help of the spatula. Cook the dish for 7 minutes at 365 F. When the time is over – stir the side dish carefully. Serve it warm. Enjoy!

Nutrition: calories 84, fat 2.9, fiber 1.4, carbs 7, protein 2.9

Eggplant Stew

Prep time: 10 minutes
Cooking time: 13 minutes
Servings: 7

Ingredients:

- 1 eggplant
- 1 zucchini
- 1 onion
- 1 green pepper
- 2 garlic cloves, peeled
- 1 teaspoon turmeric
- 1 teaspoon paprika
- 1 teaspoon dried dill
- 1 teaspoon dried parsley
- 1 cup chicken stock
- ½ cup heavy cream
- 1 teaspoon kosher salt

Directions:

Cut the zucchini and eggplant into the cubes. Then sprinkle the vegetables with the dried parsley, dried dill, paprika, and turmeric. Chop the garlic cloves. Then chop the onion and green pepper. Preheat the air fryer to 390 F. Pour the chicken stock into the air fryer and add the eggplants. Cook the eggplants for 2 minutes. After this, add the chopped onion and green pepper. Then add the chopped garlic cloves and heavy cream. Cook the stew for 11 minutes more at the same temperature. After this, transfer the cooked side dish in the serving plates. Serve the meal hot. Enjoy!

Nutrition: calories 65, fat 3.6, fiber 3.5, carbs 8.1, protein 1.7

Green Bean Casserole

Prep time: 10 minutes
Cooking time: 12 minutes
Servings: 8

Ingredients:

- 1 cup green beans
- 6 oz. Cheddar cheese, shredded
- 7 oz. Parmesan cheese, shredded
- ¼ cup heavy cream
- 1 zucchini
- 1 teaspoon salt
- 1 teaspoon paprika
- ½ teaspoon cayenne pepper
- 1 tablespoon dried parsley
- 1 tablespoon butter

Directions:

Cut the zucchini into the cubes and sprinkle with the paprika and salt. Then toss the butter in the air fryer basket tray. Add the zucchini cubes in the butter. Preheat the air fryer to 400 F and cook the zucchini for 6 minutes. Then add the green beans, shredded Cheddar cheese, and cayenne pepper. After this, sprinkle the casserole with the shredded Parmesan cheese. Pour the heavy cream. Cook the casserole for 6 minutes more at 400 F. When the casserole is cooked – let it chill well. Then transfer it to the serving plates and serve with the meat main dish. Enjoy!

Nutrition: calories 201, fat 15.3, fiber 0.9, carbs 3.3, protein 14

Cabbage Steaks

Prep time: 10 minutes
Cooking time: 5 minutes
Servings: 4

Ingredients:

- 9 oz. white cabbage, sliced
- 1 teaspoon salt
- 1 teaspoon butter
- 1 teaspoon olive oil
- 1 teaspoon paprika
- ½ teaspoon ground black pepper

Directions:

Combine the olive oil and paprika together. Melt the butter and add it to the olive oil mixture. After this, add the ground black pepper and churn it. Rub the sliced white cabbage with the spice mixture well. Then sprinkle the white cabbage slices with the salt. Preheat the air fryer to 400 F. Put the cabbage slices in the air fryer rack and cook the dish for 3 minutes. After this, turn the cabbage slices to another side and cook for 2 minutes more. When the cabbage slices are cooked – they will have light brown surface. Serve the side dish immediately. Enjoy!

Nutrition: calories 37, fat 2.3, fiber 1.9, carbs 4.2, protein 0.9

Creamed Spinach

Prep time: 10 minutes
Cooking time: 11 minutes
Servings: 6

Ingredients:

- 2 cups spinach
- 1 cup cream
- 2 tablespoon butter
- ¼ cup coconut milk
- 1 oz. walnuts, crushed
- 5 oz. Cheddar cheese, shredded
- 1 teaspoon salt

Directions:

Wash the spinach and chop it. Sprinkle the spinach with the salt and mix it up to let the spinach gives the juice. Then preheat the air fryer to 380 F. Put the spinach in the air fryer basket tray. Add the coconut milk, crushed walnuts, butter, and cream. Cook the spinach for 8 minutes. After this, stir the spinach using the wooden spatula. Add the shredded cheese and cook it for 3 minutes more. When the time is over – mix the melted cheese and spinach carefully. Serve it!

Nutrition: calories 209, fat 19.1, fiber 0.8, carbs 2.9, protein 7.9

Sriracha Broccoli

Prep time: 10 minutes
Cooking time: 6 minutes
Servings: 5

Ingredients:

- 1 teaspoon sriracha
- 1 tablespoon canola oil
- 1 teaspoon flax seeds
- 1 teaspoon ground white pepper
- 1 teaspoon kosher salt
- 1-pound broccoli
- 4 tablespoons chicken stock

Directions:

Wash the broccoli and separate it into the florets. Then combine the chicken stock, ground white pepper, flax seeds, and sriracha. Add the canola oil and whisk the mixture. Preheat the air fryer to 400 F. Put the broccoli florets in the air fryer basket rack and sprinkle the vegetables with the sriracha mixture, Cook the broccoli for 6 minutes. When the time is over – shake the broccoli gently and transfer it to the serving plates. Enjoy!

Nutrition: calories 61, fat 3.3, fiber 2.6, carbs 6.7, protein 2.7

Cheddar Cheese Sliced Cauliflower

Prep time: 15 minutes
Cooking time: 11 minutes
Servings: 7

Ingredients:
- 14 oz. cauliflower
- 6 oz. Cheddar cheese, sliced
- 1 teaspoon salt
- 1 teaspoon ground black pepper
- 1 teaspoon butter, frozen
- 1 teaspoon dried dill
- 1 tablespoon olive oil

Directions:

Wash the cauliflower head carefully and slice it into the servings. Sprinkle the sliced cauliflower with the salt, ground black pepper, and dried dill. Grate the frozen butter. Then sprinkle the cauliflower with the olive oil from the both sides. Preheat the air fryer to 400 F. Place the cauliflower slices in the air fryer rack and cook it for 7 minutes. After this, turn the cauliflower slices into another side and sprinkle them with the grated frozen butter. Cook the cauliflower for 3 minutes more. Then place the cheese slices over the cauliflower and cook it for 1 minute more. Transfer the cooked cauliflower to the serving plates with the help of the spatula. Serve the dish immediately. Enjoy!

Nutrition: calories 135, fat 10.7, fiber 1.5, carbs 3.6, protein 7.2

Mexican Zucchini

Prep time: 10 minutes
Cooking time: 12 minutes
Servings: 8

Ingredients:
- 3 zucchini
- 1 tablespoon canola oil
- ½ teaspoon chili powder
- 1 teaspoon garlic powder
- 6 oz. Cheddar cheese, shredded

Directions:

Cut the zucchini into the cubes. Sprinkle the zucchini cubes with eth chili powder, garlic powder, and olive oil. Then preheat the air fryer to 400 F. Place the zucchini cubes in the air fryer and cook the vegetables for 10 minutes. Then sprinkle the zucchini with the shredded cheese. Cook the side dish for 2 minutes more. When the zucchini is cooked – transfer the dish to the serving plates. Enjoy!

Nutrition: calories 115, fat 9, fiber 0.9, carbs 3.1, protein 6.3

Wrapped Bacon Asparagus

Prep time: 15 minutes
Cooking time: 10 minutes
Servings: 6

Ingredients:
- 7 oz. bacon, sliced
- 14 oz. asparagus
- 1 teaspoon salt
- 1 teaspoon ground black pepper
- 1 tablespoon sesame oil
- 1 teaspoon paprika

Directions:

Wrap the asparagus in the sliced bacon. Preheat the air fryer to 380 F. Put the wrapped asparagus in the air fryer and sprinkle the vegetables with the salt, ground black pepper, paprika, and sesame oil. Cook the asparagus for 5 minutes. After this, turn the asparagus to another side and cook it for 5 minutes more. Then transfer the cooked dish in the serving plates. Serve the side dish only hot. Enjoy!

Nutrition: calories 214, fat 16.2, fiber 1.6, carbs 3.5, protein 13.8

Stuffed Artichoke with Spinach

Prep time: 15 minutes
Cooking time: 40 minutes
Servings: 5

Ingredients:
- 4 tablespoons fresh spinach, chopped
- ½ tablespoon heavy cream
- 1 teaspoon butter
- 1 teaspoon salt
- 1-pound artichoke
- 1 teaspoon olive oil
- ½ lemon
- 1 teaspoon ground black pepper

Directions:

Prepare the artichokes and remove the heart from them. Then combine the chopped spinach with the heavy cream and butter. Mix the mixture up. After this, rub the artichokes with the salt, olive oil, ground black pepper, and a half of the lemon. Fill the artichokes with the spinach cream mixture. Then wrap the artichokes in the foil. Preheat the air fryer to 350 F. Put the wrapped artichokes in the air fryer basket and cook them for 40 minutes. When the time is over and artichokes are cooked - discard them from the air fryer. Remove the foil and serve the side dish immediately. Enjoy!

Nutrition: calories 66, fat 2.4, fiber 5.2, carbs 10.4, protein 3.2

Shredded Brussel Sprouts

Prep time: 10 minutes
Cooking time: 15 minutes
Servings: 6

Ingredients:

- 17 oz. Brussel sprouts
- 1 oz. butter
- 1 tablespoon olive oil
- 1 teaspoon ground white pepper
- 1 teaspoon salt
- 1 tablespoon apple cider vinegar

Directions:

Place the Brussel sprouts in the blender and shred them. Then preheat the air fryer to 380 F. Put the shredded Brussel sprouts in the air fryer basket tray. Add the butter, olive oil, ground white pepper, salt, and apple cider vinegar. Mix the shredded Brussel sprouts carefully with the help of the spoon. Cook the dish in the preheated air fryer for 15 minutes. When the time is over – remove the dish from the air fryer and stir it. Serve it immediately. Enjoy!

Nutrition: calories 90, fat 6.4, fiber 3.1, carbs 7.6, protein 2.8

Cauliflower Rice with Parmesan and Pesto

Prep time: 10 minutes
Cooking time: 13 minutes
Servings: 7

Ingredients:

- 1-pound cauliflower head
- 2 tablespoon pesto sauce
- 6 oz. Parmesan, shredded
- 1 teaspoon salt
- 1 teaspoon olive oil
- ½ cup heavy cream
- 1 tablespoon butter
- 1 tablespoon dried dill
- 1 teaspoon dried parsley
- 1 teaspoon chili flakes

Directions:

Wash the cauliflower head carefully and chop it roughly. Place the chopped cauliflower in the blender and blend it well until you get the texture of the cauliflower rice. Then place the cauliflower rice in the air fryer and sprinkle it with the salt, olive oil, butter, dried dill, dried parsley, and chili flakes. Mix the cauliflower rice carefully with the help of the wooden spatula. After this, add the heavy cream and cook the dish at 370 F for 10 minutes. After this, add shredded Parmesan and pesto sauce. Mix the cauliflower rice carefully and cook it for 3 minutes more at the same temperature. Serve the side dish immediately. Enjoy!

Nutrition: calories 165, fat 12.6, fiber 1.8, carbs 5.1, protein 9.8

Air Fryer Bok Choy

Prep time: 10 minutes
Cooking time: 10 minutes
Servings: 6

Ingredients:

- 1 white onion, sliced
- 1-pound bok choy
- 1 teaspoon minced garlic
- 1 tablespoon mustard
- 1 teaspoon ground ginger
- 2 tablespoon apple cider vinegar
- 2 teaspoons olive oil
- 1 tablespoon butter

Directions:

Wash the bok choy and chop it. Then place the chopped bok choy in the air fryer basket tray. Sprinkle the chopped bok choy with the minced garlic, sliced onion, mustard, ground ginger, apple cider vinegar, olive oil, and butter. Preheat the air fryer to 360 F. Cook the bok choy for 10 minutes. When the dish is cooked – stir it carefully. Then let the cooked dish cool little. Serve it and enjoy!

Nutrition: calories 59, fat 4.2, fiber 1.5, carbs 4.4, protein 1.9

Garlic Green Peppers

Prep time: 10 minutes
Cooking time: 15 minutes
Servings: 4

Ingredients:

- 1 teaspoon minced garlic
- 1-pound green pepper
- 1 teaspoon salt
- 1 tablespoon olive oil

Directions:

Wash the green peppers carefully and remove the seeds from them. After this, cut the green peppers into the medium squares. Preheat the air fryer to 320 F. Then place the green pepper squares in the big mixing bowl. Sprinkle the green peppers with the olive oil, salt, and minced garlic. Mix it up. Place the prepared green peppers in the air fryer basket tray. Cook the dish for 15 minutes. Stir the green peppers after 8 minutes of the cooking. Serve the side dish when it is chilled – get the room temperature. Enjoy!

Nutrition: calories 54, fat 0.6, fiber 1.9, carbs 5.5, protein 1

Zucchini Boats with Cheese

Prep time: 15 minutes
Cooking time: 12 minutes
Servings: 4

Ingredients:

- 1 medium zucchini
- 3 oz bok choy
- 1 garlic clove, sliced
- 6 oz. Cheddar cheese
- 4 tablespoons heavy cream
- 1 tablespoon coconut flour
- ¼ teaspoon salt
- ½ teaspoon ground black pepper
- 1 teaspoon paprika
- 1 teaspoon olive oil

Directions:

Cut the zucchini into 2 parts crosswise. Then remove the flesh from the zucchini halves. Blend the zucchini flesh and combine it with the sliced garlic clove. After this, sprinkle the zucchini flesh with the salt, ground black pepper, and paprika. Mix it up. Combine the heavy cream and coconut flour and whisk the liquid. Fill the zucchini halves with the zucchini flesh mixture. Grind the bok choy and sprinkle it with the heavy cream mixture. Shred Cheddar cheese. Add the bok choy mixture in the zucchini halves. Then sprinkle the zucchini with the olive oil. Preheat the air fryer to 400 F. Put the zucchini halves in the air fryer and cook them for 10 minutes. Then sprinkle the zucchini boards with the shredded cheese and cook for 2 minutes more. After this, transfer the cooked zucchini boards in the plate and chill them little. Cut every zucchini half into 2 parts more. Serve it!

Nutrition: calories 255, fat 21.2, fiber 1.8, carbs 5, protein 12.2

Parsley Butter Mushrooms

Prep time: 10 minutes
Cooking time: 7 minutes
Servings: 5

Ingredients:

- 10 oz. white mushrooms
- 1 white onion, sliced
- 1 teaspoon olive oil
- 1/3 teaspoon garlic powder
- 3 tablespoon butter
- ½ cup heavy cream
- 2 tablespoon dried parsley
- ½ teaspoon salt

Directions:

Slice the white mushrooms and sprinkle them with the garlic powder and salt. Preheat the air fryer to 400 F. Put the sliced mushrooms in the air fryer basket tray. Sprinkle the mushrooms with the olive oil. Add sliced white onion. Cook the mushrooms for 2 minutes. Then stir the sliced mushrooms carefully. Add the butter and heavy cream. Sprinkle the mushrooms with the dried parsley. Stir the mushrooms carefully and cook them for 5 minutes more. When the time is over – stir the cooked dish carefully. Serve it!

Nutrition: calories 133, fat 12.5, fiber 1.1, carbs 4.5, protein 2.4

Zucchini Noodles

Prep time: 15 minutes
Cooking time: 5 minutes
Servings: 4

Ingredients:

- 1 green zucchini
- 1 cup chicken stock
- 1 teaspoon butter
- ½ teaspoon salt
- ½ teaspoon ground white pepper

Directions:

Preheat the air fryer to 400 F. Make the zucchini noodles using the spiralizer. Pour the chicken stock into the air fryer basket tray. Add chicken stock, salt, and ground white pepper. Cook the zucchini stock for 2 minutes. After this, add the zucchini noodles and cook them for 3 minutes. Then strain the chicken stock and add butter. Mix the zucchini noodles gentle not to damage them. Serve the side dish and enjoy!

Nutrition: calories 19, fat 1.2, fiber 0.6, carbs 2, protein 0.8

Butter Mashed Cauliflower

Prep time: 10 minutes
Cooking time: 13 minutes
Servings: 5

Ingredients:

- 2 tablespoons butter
- 4 tablespoons heavy cream
- 1-pound cauliflower
- 1 teaspoon garlic powder
- ½ teaspoon salt
- 1 teaspoon ground chili pepper
- 1 teaspoon olive oil

Directions:

Preheat the air fryer to 360 F. Chop the cauliflower roughly and place it in the air fryer basket tray. Sprinkle the vegetables with the garlic powder, salt, ground chili pepper, and olive oil. Cook the cauliflower for 10 minutes. After this, stir the cauliflower gently, add the heavy cream, and cook it for 3 minutes more at 390 F. Then transfer the cooked soft cauliflower in the blender. Blend it well till you get the soft and smooth texture. Add the butter and stir it carefully. Serve the mashed cauliflower hot or warm. Enjoy!

Nutrition: calories 115, fat 10.1, fiber 2.3, carbs 5.6, protein 2.2

Crab Mushrooms

Prep time: 15 minutes
Cooking time: 5 minutes
Servings: 5

Ingredients:

- 7 oz. crab meat
- 10 oz. white mushrooms
- ½ teaspoon salt
- ¼ cup fish stock
- 1 teaspoon butter
- ¼ teaspoon ground coriander
- 1 teaspoon dried cilantro
- 1 teaspoon butter

Directions:

Chop the crab meat and sprinkle it with the salt and dried cilantro. Mix the crab meat carefully. Preheat the air fryer to 400 F. Chop the white mushrooms and combine them with the crab meat. After this, add the fish stock, ground coriander, and butter. Transfer the side dish mixture in the air fryer basket tray. Stir it gently with the help of the plastic spatula. Cook the side dish for 5 minutes. When the time is over – let the dish rest for 5 minutes. Then serve it. Enjoy!

Nutrition: calories 56, fat 1.7, fiber 0.6, carbs 2.6, protein 7

Soft Bacon Cabbage

Prep time: 10 minutes
Cooking time: 15 minutes
Servings: 4

Ingredients:

- 4 oz. bacon, chopped
- 10 oz. white cabbage, shredded
- ¼ white onion, diced
- ½ teaspoon salt
- 1 teaspoon paprika
- 1 teaspoon butter
- ½ teaspoon ground black pepper

Directions:

Preheat the air fryer to 360 F. Put the chopped bacon in the air fryer basket tray. Sprinkle it with the salt and paprika. Add butter and cook the bacon for 8 minutes. After this, add the shredded cabbage, diced onion, butter, and ground black pepper. Stir the mixture carefully and cook it for 7 minutes more. When the time is over and the cabbage is soft stir the side dish carefully. Serve it hot and enjoy!

Nutrition: calories 184, fat 13, fiber 2.2, carbs 5.6, protein 11.6

Eggplant Salad with White Mushrooms

Prep time: 20 minutes
Cooking time: 23 minutes
Servings: 6

Ingredients:

- 1 cup water
- 1 eggplant
- 6 oz. white mushrooms
- 1 garlic clove, sliced
- 2 tablespoon apple cider vinegar
- 1 tablespoon olive oil
- 1 teaspoon canola oil
- ½ tablespoon flax seeds
- 1 teaspoon ground black pepper
- 1 teaspoon salt

Directions:

Peel the eggplant and cut it into the medium cubes. Then sprinkle the eggplant cubes with the ½ teaspoon of salt. Stir the eggplant cubes gently and leave them for 5 minutes. Meanwhile, chop the white mushrooms. Preheat the air fryer to 400 F. Pour water in the air fryer basket tray. Add the chopped mushrooms, ½ teaspoon salt, and cook them for 8 minutes. Then strain water from the mushrooms and chill them. Then place the eggplant cubes in the air fryer and sprinkle them with the canola oil. Cook the eggplants for 15 minutes at 400 F. Stir the eggplants after 7 minutes of the cooking. When the eggplants are cooked – let them chill little. Combine the eggplants with the chopped mushrooms in the salad bowl. Sprinkle the dish with the flax seeds, olive oil, sliced garlic clove, and ground black pepper. After this, add the apple cider vinegar and stir the salad carefully. Let the salad rest for 5 minutes. Serve it or keep in the fridge. Enjoy!

Nutrition: calories 62, fat 3.5, fiber 3.8, carbs 6.9, protein 2

Garlic Zucchini Pate

Prep time: 15 minutes
Cooking time: 12 minutes
Servings: 4

Ingredients:

- 2 garlic cloves, chopped
- 1 tablespoon butter
- 1 teaspoon salt
- ½ teaspoon ground black pepper
- 2 zucchini
- ½ tablespoon olive oil

Directions:

Peel the zucchini and grate it. Then combine the grated zucchini with the salt and ground black pepper. Stir the zucchini. Preheat the air fryer to 390 F. Put the grated zucchini in the air fryer basket tray, add olive oil and chopped garlic clove, and cook it for 8 minutes. Then stir the zucchini carefully and add butter. Cook the zucchini pate for 4 minutes more at 400 F. When the time is over and the zucchini pate is smooth and soft – remove it from the air fryer and chill it till the room temperature. Serve it and enjoy!

Nutrition: calories 59, fat 4.8, fiber 1.2, carbs 4, protein 1.4

Warm Broccoli Salad

Prep time: 10 minutes
Cooking time: 6 minutes
Servings: 4

Ingredients:
- 12 oz. broccoli
- 4 oz. bacon, chopped, cooked
- 1 tablespoon chives
- 1 tablespoon apple cider vinegar
- 1 teaspoon stevia extract
- 1 teaspoon flax seeds
- 1 tablespoon canola oil

Directions:
Preheat the air fryer to 400 F. Separate the broccoli into the small florets and place them in the air fryer. Sprinkle the broccoli florets with the canola oil and cook for 6 minutes. Meanwhile, sprinkle the cooked chopped bacon with the apple cider vinegar. Place the chopped bacon in the salad bowl. Add chives, flax seeds, and stevia extract. Shake the mixture gently. When the broccoli florets are cooked – transfer them to the salad bowl and stir the salad carefully. Serve it immediately. Enjoy!

Nutrition: calories 217, fat 15.8, fiber 2.4, carbs 6.3, protein 13

Chinese Greens

Prep time: 10 minutes
Cooking time: 10 minutes
Servings: 5

Ingredients:
- 1 tablespoon chives
- 1 teaspoon sesame seeds
- 1 tablespoon apple cider vinegar
- 2 tablespoon butter
- 1 tablespoon canola oil
- ½ teaspoon salt
- 8 oz bok choy
- 1 tablespoon garlic, sliced
- ½ teaspoon stevia extract

Directions:
Prehcat the air fryer to 360 F. Slice the bok choy and place it in the air fryer basket tray. Then sprinkle the sliced bok choy with the salt and butter. Cook the bok choy for 10 minutes. When the bok choy is cooked – let it chill gently and transfer to the serving bowl. Combine the chives, sesame seeds, apple cider vinegar, canola oil, and stevia extract in the shallow bowl. Add the sliced garlic and mix it. Then sprinkle the cooked bok choy with the prepared garlic mixture. Stir it gently. Serve it and enjoy!

Nutrition: calories 78, fat 7.8, fiber 0.6, carbs 1.8, protein 1

Crunchy Bacon with Brussel Sprouts

Prep time: 7 minutes
Cooking time: 20 minutes
Servings: 7

Ingredients:

- 6 oz. bacon
- 1-pound Brussel sprouts
- 1 tablespoon olive oil
- 2 tablespoon walnuts, crushed
- 1 teaspoon fresh lemon juice
- ½ teaspoon lime zest
- ½ teaspoon salt
- 2 tablespoon canola oil

Directions:

Chop the bacon. Preheat the air fryer to 360 F. Place the chopped bacon in the air fryer basket tray. Cook it for 5 minutes. After this, stir the chopped bacon carefully and cook it for 5 minutes more. Then transfer the cooked bacon to the serving bowl. Put the Brussel sprouts in the air fryer basket tray. Add canola oil and salt. Sprinkle the vegetables with the lime zest. Cook the vegetables for 15 minutes at 380 F. Sprinkle the chopped cooked bacon with the crushed walnuts. Add olive oil and fresh lemon juice. When the Brussel sprouts are cooked let them chill until the room temperature. Add the cooked vegetables in the bacon and stir it carefully. Serve it!

Nutrition: calories 226, fat 17.7, fiber 2.6, carbs 6.5, protein 11.8

Turnip Mash

Prep time: 10 minutes
Cooking time: 14 minutes
Servings: 6

Ingredients:

- 5 turnips
- 3 oz. butter
- ½ white onion, grated
- 1 teaspoon salt
- 1 cup heavy cream

Directions:

Preheat the air fryer to 400 F. Peel the turnips and chop them. Place the chopped turnips in the air fryer basket tray. Add butter, grated onion, salt, and heavy cream. Cook the dish for 14 minutes. When the time is over and the turnip is cooked – let it chill for 5 minutes. After this, blend the turnip mixture into the mash. Use the hand blender for this step. Serve the cooked turnip mash warm. Add more salt if desired. Enjoy!

Nutrition: calories 203, fat 19, fiber 2, carbs 8, protein 1.6

Fragrant Daikon

Prep time: 10 minutes
Cooking time: 10 minutes
Servings: 5

Ingredients:

- 1-pound daikon
- ½ teaspoon sage
- 1 teaspoon salt
- 1 tablespoon olive oil
- 1 teaspoon dried oregano

Directions:

Peel the daikon and cut it into the cubes. Sprinkle the daikon cubes with the sage, salt, and dried oregano. Mix it up. Preheat the air fryer to 360 F. Place the daikon cubes in the air fryer rack and sprinkle the vegetables with the olive oil. Cook the daikon for 6 minutes. After this, turn the daikon cubes to another side and cook the dish for 4 minutes more. When the time is over – the daikon cubes should be soft and little bit golden brown. Serve the cooked side dish immediately. Enjoy!

Nutrition: calories 43, fat 2.8, fiber 2, carbs 3.9, protein 1.9

Green Cream Mass

Prep time: 10 minutes
Cooking time: 12 minutes
Servings: 4

Ingredients:

- ½ white onion, grated
- 2 cup spinach
- 1 cup chicken stock
- 1 cup heavy cream
- 1 teaspoon salt
- 1 teaspoon paprika
- ½ teaspoon chili flakes
- 1 teaspoon ground black pepper
- ½ teaspoon minced garlic
- 3 oz. Parmesan, shredded

Directions:

Preheat the air fryer to 390 F. Chop the spinach into the small pieces. Place the spinach in the air fryer basket bowl. Add the chicken stock and heavy cream. After this, add salt, paprika, chili flakes, and ground black pepper. Add the grated white onion and minced garlic. Mix the soup mixture gently and cook it for 10 minutes. When the time is over and the soup is cooked – blend it well with the help of the hand blender. You should get the creamy texture of the soup. Sprinkle the cream mass with the shredded cheese and cook it for 2 minutes at 400 F. Serve it hot!

Nutrition: calories 187, fat 16, fiber 1, carbs 4.4, protein 8.4

Eggplant Circles with Grated Cheese

Prep time: 15 minutes
Cooking time: 11 minutes
Servings: 7

Ingredients:

- 2 eggplants
- 1 teaspoon minced garlic
- 1 teaspoon olive oil
- 5 oz. Cheddar cheese, grated
- ½ teaspoon ground black pepper

Directions:

Wash the eggplants carefully and slice them. Rub the eggplant slices with the minced garlic, salt, and ground black pepper. Leave the eggplant slices for 5 minutes to marinate. After this, preheat an air fryer to 400 F. Place the eggplant circles in the air fryer rack and cook them for 6 minutes. Then turn the eggplant circles to another side and cook for 5 minutes more. Sprinkle the eggplants with the grated cheese and cook for 30 seconds more. Serve the cooked side dish immediately. Enjoy!

Nutrition: calories 127, fat 7.7, fiber 5.6, carbs 9.7, protein 6.6

Air Fryer Garlic Heads

Prep time: 7 minutes
Cooking time: 10 minutes
Servings: 8

Ingredients:

- 1-pound garlic heads
- 2 tablespoons olive oil
- 1 teaspoon dried oregano
- 1 teaspoon dried basil
- 1 teaspoon ground coriander
- ¼ teaspoon ground ginger

Directions:

Cut the ends of the garlic heads. Place each garlic head on the foil. Then sprinkle the garlic heads with the olive oil, dried oregano, dried basil, ground coriander, and ground ginger. Preheat the air fryer to 400 F. Wrap the garlic heads in the foil and place them in the air fryer. Cook the garlic heads for 10 minutes. When the time is over – the garlic heads should be soft. Let them cool for at least 10 minutes. Serve the dish immediately. Enjoy!

Nutrition: calories 115, fat 3.8, fiber 1.3, carbs 17.9, protein 3.6

Short Parmesan Sticks

Prep time: 10 minutes
Cooking time: 8 minutes
Servings: 3

Ingredients:

- 8 oz. Parmesan
- 1 egg
- ½ cup heavy cream
- 4 tablespoons almond flour
- ¼ teaspoon ground black pepper

Directions:

Beat the egg in the bowl and whisk it. Add the heavy cream and almond flour. Then sprinkle the mixture with the ground black pepper. Whisk it carefully or use the hand mixer. After this, cut the cheese into the thick short sticks Dip the cheese sticks in the heavy cream mixture. Then place the cheese sticks in the plastic bags and freeze them. Preheat the air fryer to 400 F. Place the cheese sticks in the air fryer rack. Cook the cheese sticks for 8 minutes. When the time is over – the sticks are cooked. Transfer the dish to the serving plate. Enjoy!

Nutrition: calories 389, fat 29.5, fiber 1.1, carbs 5.5, protein 28.6

Creamy Snow Peas

Prep time: 7 minutes
Cooking time: 5 minutes
Servings: 4

Ingredients:

- ½ cup heavy cream
- 1 teaspoon butter
- 1 teaspoon salt
- 1 teaspoon paprika
- 1-pound snow peas
- ¼ teaspoon nutmeg

Directions:

Preheat the air fryer to 400 F. Wash the snow peas carefully and place them in the air fryer basket tray. Then sprinkle the snow peas with the butter, salt, paprika, nutmeg, and heavy cream. Cook the snow peas for 5 minutes. When the time is over – shake the snow peas gently and transfer them to the serving plates. Enjoy!

Nutrition: calories 110, fat 6.9, fiber 3.4, carbs 8.8, protein 4.1

Sesame Okra

Prep time: 8 minutes
Cooking time: 4 minutes
Servings: 4

Ingredients:

- 1 tablespoon sesame oil
- 1 teaspoon sesame seed
- 11 oz. okra
- ½ teaspoon salt
- 1 egg

Directions:

Wash the okra and chop it roughly. Crack the egg into the bowl and whisk it. Add the whisked egg in the chopped okra. Sprinkle it with the sesame seeds and salt. Preheat the air fryer to 400 F. Mix the okra mixture carefully. Place the okra mixture in the air fryer basket. Sprinkle it with the olive oil. Cook the okra for 4 minutes. When the time is over – stir the cooked dish. Transfer it to the serving plates. Enjoy!

Nutrition: calories 81, fat 5, fiber 2.6, carbs 6.1, protein 3

Fennel Wedges

Prep time: 15 minutes
Cooking time: 6 minutes
Servings: 5

Ingredients:

- 1 teaspoon stevia extract
- ½ teaspoon fresh thyme
- ½ teaspoon salt
- 1 teaspoon canola oil
- 14 oz. fennel
- 1 teaspoon butter
- 1 teaspoon dried oregano
- ½ teaspoon chili flakes

Directions:

Slice the fennel into the wedges. Melt the butter. Combine the butter, canola oil, dried oregano, and chili flakes in the bowl. Churn the mixture. Add salt, fresh thyme, and stevia extract. Whisk it gently. Then brush the fennel wedges with the churned mixture. Preheat the air fryer to 370 F. Place the fennel wedges in the air fryer rack. Cook the fennel wedges for 3 minutes from each side. When the fennel wedges are cooked – transfer them directly to the serving plates. Enjoy!

Nutrition: calories 41, fat 1.9, fiber 2.6, carbs 6.1, protein 1

Kohlrabi Fritters

Prep time: 10 minutes
Cooking time: 7 minutes
Servings: 5

Ingredients:

- 8 oz. kohlrabi
- 1 egg
- 1 tablespoon almond flour
- ½ teaspoon salt
- 1 teaspoon olive oil
- 1 teaspoon ground black pepper
- 1 tablespoon dried parsley
- ¼ teaspoon chili pepper

Directions:

Peel the kohlrabi and grate it. Combine the grated kohlrabi with the salt, ground black pepper, dried parsley, and chili pepper. Beat the egg into the mixture and whisk it. After this, make the medium fritters from the mixture. Preheat the air fryer to 380 F. Spray the air fryer basket tray with the olive oil inside and place the fritters there. Cook the fritters for 4 minutes. After this, turn the fritters to another side and cook them for 3 minutes more. When the fritters are cooked – let them chill gently. Serve the dish!

Nutrition: calories 66, fat 4.7, fiber 2.4, carbs 4.4, protein 3.2

Delightful Bamboo Shoots

Prep time: 8 minutes
Cooking time: 4 minutes
Servings: 2

Ingredients:

- 8 oz. bamboo shoots
- 2 garlic cloves, sliced
- 1 tablespoon olive oil
- ½ teaspoon chili flakes
- 2 tablespoon chives
- ½ teaspoon salt
- 3 tablespoons fish stock

Directions:

Preheat the air fryer to 400 F. Cut the bamboo shoots into the strips. Combine the sliced garlic cloves, olive oil, chili flakes, salt, and fish stock in the air fryer basket tray. Cook it for 1 minute. After this, stir the mixture gently. Add the bamboo shoots strips and chives. Stir the dish carefully and cook it for 3 minutes more. Then stir the cooked side dish carefully. Transfer it to the serving plates. Serve the dish with the ground meat. Enjoy!

Nutrition: calories 100, fat 7.6, fiber 2.6, carbs 7, protein 3.7

Keto Summer Vegetables

Prep time: 15 minutes
Cooking time: 15 minutes
Servings: 4

Ingredients:

- 1 eggplant
- 1 tomato
- 1 zucchini
- 1 white onion
- 2 green peppers

- 1 teaspoon paprika
- 1 tablespoon canola oil
- ½ teaspoon ground nutmeg
- ½ teaspoon ground thyme
- 1 teaspoon salt

Directions:

Preheat the air fryer to 390 F. Wash the eggplant, tomato, and zucchini carefully. Peel the onion. Chop all the prepared vegetables roughly. Then place the chopped vegetables in the air fryer basket tray. Sprinkle the vegetables with the paprika, canola oil, ground nutmeg, ground thyme, and salt. Stir the vegetables carefully with the help of two spatulas. Cut the green peppers into the squares. Add the pepper squares into the vegetable mixture. Stir it gently. Cook the dish for 15 minutes. Stir the vegetables after 10 minutes carefully. When the vegetables are cooked – let them chill for 4 minutes. Serve the dish!

Nutrition: calories 96, fat 4.1, fiber 6.7, carbs 14.8, protein 2.8

Zucchini Hasselback

Prep time: 15 minutes
Cooking time: 12 minutes
Servings: 2

Ingredients:

- 1 zucchini
- 4 oz. Cheddar, sliced
- ½ teaspoon salt
- ½ teaspoon dried oregano
- ½ teaspoon ground coriander

- ½ teaspoon paprika
- 3 tablespoons heavy cream
- 1 teaspoon olive oil
- ¼ teaspoon minced garlic

Directions:

Cut the zucchini in the shape of the Hasselback. Then fill the zucchini with the sliced cheese. Sprinkle the zucchini Hasselback with the salt, dried oregano, ground coriander, paprika, minced garlic, olive oil, and heavy cream. Preheat the air fryer to 400 F. Wrap the zucchini Hasselback in the foil and place in the preheated air fryer. Cook the dish for 12 minutes. When the zucchini is cooked – discard it from the foil and cut into 2 parts. Serve it!

Nutrition: calories 215, fat 14.9, fiber 1.5, carbs 5.7, protein 15.6

Rutabaga Hash

Prep time: 10 minutes
Cooking time: 14 minutes
Servings: 3

Ingredients:

- 1 cup chicken stock
- 10 oz. rutabaga
- 1 teaspoon salt
- 1 tablespoon butter
- 1 teaspoon dried dill
- ¼ teaspoon paprika

Directions:

Peel the rutabaga and chop it. Then preheat the air fryer to 370 F. Pour the chicken stock into the air fryer basket tray. Add salt, chopped rutabaga, butter, dried dill, and paprika. Stir it gently. Cook the rutabaga for 14 minutes. When the dish is cooked – transfer it to the bowl. Use the fork to make a mash. When the rutabaga mash is homogenous – serve it immediately. Enjoy!

Nutrition: calories 73, fat 4.3, fiber 2.5, carbs 8.2, protein 1.5

Butter Sliced Mushrooms with Onion

Prep time: 10 minutes
Cooking time: 10 minutes
Servings: 2

Ingredients:

- 1 cup white mushrooms
- 1 white onion
- 1 tablespoon butter
- 1 teaspoon olive oil
- 1 teaspoon dried rosemary
- 1/3 teaspoon salt
- ¼ teaspoon ground nutmeg

Directions:

Preheat the air fryer to 400 F. Pour the olive oil and butter in the air fryer basket tray. Add the dried rosemary, salt, and ground nutmeg. Stir it gently. Peel the onion and slice it. Add the sliced onion in the air fryer basket tray. Cook the onion for 5 minutes. Meanwhile, chop the white mushrooms. Add the white mushrooms after 5 minutes of the cooking of the onion. Stir the mixture and cook it for 5 minutes more at the same temperature. When the dish is cooked – stir it carefully. Enjoy!

Nutrition: calories 104, fat 8.4, fiber 1.9, carbs 6.8, protein 1.8

Fennel Quiche

Prep time: 15 minutes
Cooking time: 18 minutes
Servings: 4

Ingredients:

- 10 oz. fennel, chopped
- 1 cup spinach
- 5 eggs
- ½ cup almond flour
- 1 teaspoon olive oil
- 1 tablespoon butter
- 1 teaspoon salt
- ¼ cup heavy cream
- 1 teaspoon ground black pepper

Directions:

Chop the spinach and combine it with the chopped fennel in the big bowl. Beat the egg in the separate bowl and whisk them. Combine the whisked eggs with the almond flour, butter, salt, heavy cream, and ground black pepper. Whisk it. Preheat the air fryer to 360 F. Spray the air fryer basket tray with the olive oil inside. Then add the spinach-fennel mixture and pour the whisked egg mixture. Cook the quiche for 18 minutes. When the time is over – let the quiche chill little. Then remove it from the air fryer and slice into the servings. Enjoy!

Nutrition: calories 249, fat 19.1, fiber 4, carbs 9.4, protein 11.3

Snacks and Appetizers

Cauliflower Crispy Florets

Prep time: 15 minutes
Cooking time: 16 minutes
Servings: 8

Ingredients:

- 18 oz. cauliflower
- 1 cup heavy cream
- 1 teaspoon salt
- ½ teaspoon ground black pepper
- 1 teaspoon turmeric
- 1 egg
- 2 tablespoons almond flour
- 1 teaspoon oregano
- ½ tablespoon olive oil

Directions:

Wash the cauliflower carefully and separate it into the medium florets. After this beat the egg in the big bowl and whisk it. Add the salt, ground black pepper, turmeric, almond flour, and oregano. Whisk the mixture till you get the smooth batter. Then coat the cauliflower florets with the heavy cream batter. Preheat the air fryer to 360 F. Place the coated cauliflower in the air fryer basket tray. Cook the vegetables for 12 minutes. After this, increase the temperature to 390 F and cook the snack for 4 minutes more. Chill the cooked cauliflower florets. Serve it!

Nutrition: calories 125, fat 10.6, fiber 2.5, carbs 5.7, protein 3.8

Scotch Eggs

Prep time: 15 minutes
Cooking time: 13 minutes
Servings: 3

Ingredients:

- 3 eggs, boiled
- ½ cup coconut flour
- 1 egg
- 16 oz. ground beef
- 1 teaspoon salt
- 1 teaspoon ground black pepper
- 1 teaspoon turmeric
- 1 teaspoon olive oil

Directions:

Beat the egg in the bowl and whisk it. Then peel the boiled eggs. Combine the ground beef with the salt, ground black pepper, and turmeric. Mix the mixture up. Make 3 balls from the ground beef mixture and put the boiled eggs inside to make the round meatballs. Then dip the meatballs in the whisked egg. After this, coat the meatballs in the coconut flour generously. Preheat the air fryer to 370 F. Place the scotch eggs there and spray them with the olive oil. Cook the dish for 10 minutes. After this, increase the temperature to 380 F and cook the dish for 3 minutes more. When the scotch eggs are cooked – chill them for at least 2-3 minutes. Enjoy!

Nutrition: calories 318, fat 12.7, fiber 8.3, carbs 14.5, protein 35.3

Eggplants Circles

Prep time: 15 minutes
Cooking time: 8 minutes
Servings: 7

Ingredients:

- 2 eggplants
- 1 tablespoon canola oil
- 1 teaspoon minced garlic
- ½ teaspoon salt
- 1 teaspoon ground turmeric
- 1 teaspoon dried rosemary

Directions:

Wash the eggplants carefully and slice into the thick circles. After this, combine the canola oil, minced garlic, salt, ground turmeric, and dried rosemary in the bowl. Churn the mixture. After this, brush every eggplants circle with the oil mixture. Preheat the air fryer to 400 F. Place the prepared eggplants circles in the air fryer rack and cook them for 5 minutes. After this, turn the eggplant circles to another side and cook them for 3 minutes more. When the eggplants are soft and little bit golden brown – they are cooked. Let them chill till the room temperature. Serve the dish!

Nutrition: calories 59, fat 2.3, fiber 5.7, carbs 9.7, protein 1.6

Onion Circles

Prep time: 15 minutes
Cooking time: 8 minutes
Servings: 10

Ingredients:

- 2 white onions
- ½ teaspoon salt
- ½ cup coconut flour
- ½ teaspoon paprika
- ½ teaspoon ground black pepper
- 1 egg
- 1/3 cup heavy cream
- 1/3 cup almond flour
- 1 tablespoon olive oil

Directions:

Peel the white onions and slice them roughly. Then separate the sliced onions into the circles. Beat the egg and whisk it. Sprinkle the whisked egg with the paprika, salt, ground black pepper, and heavy cream. Whisk it well until homogenous. Preheat the air fryer to 360 F. Coat the onion rings in the almond flour. After this, dip the onion circles in the whisked egg mixture. Then coat the onion circles in the coconut flour. Spray the air fryer basket tray with the olive oil and place the onion circles there. Cook the onion circles for 8 minutes. When the snack is cooked – let it chill well. Enjoy!

Nutrition: calories 88, fat 5.7, fiber 3.3, carbs 7.1, protein 2.5

Zucchini Fritters

Prep time: 10 minutes
Cooking time: 10 minutes
Servings: 7

Ingredients:

- 1 zucchini, grated
- 1 egg
- 4 tablespoons coconut flour
- ½ teaspoon salt
- ½ tablespoon paprika
- 1 teaspoon butter
- ¼ onion, grated
- ½ teaspoon chili flakes

Directions:

Put the grated zucchini in the big mixing bowl. Beat the egg in the zucchini. Then add coconut flour, salt, paprika, grated onion, and chili flakes. Mix the mixture carefully. Preheat the air fryer to 365 F. Put the butter in the air fryer basket tray and melt it. After this, make the small fritters with the help of the spoon and place them in the melted butter. Cook the fritters for 5 minutes from each side. When the fritters are cooked – chill them well. Enjoy!

Nutrition: calories 38, fat 1.7, fiber 2.3, carbs 4.5, protein 1.8

Chicken Bites

Prep time: 15 minutes
Cooking time: 15 minutes
Servings: 8

Ingredients:

- 1-pound chicken fillet
- 1 teaspoon chili flakes
- 1 teaspoon turmeric
- 1 teaspoon paprika
- ½ teaspoon curry powder
- ½ cup heavy cream
- 2 tablespoons almond flour
- 1 teaspoon olive oil

Directions:

Chop the chicken fillet into 8 cubes. Place the chicken cubes in the big bowl. Then sprinkle the meat with the chili flakes, turmeric, paprika, and curry powder. Mix the meat up with the help of the hands. After this, combine the heavy cream and almond flour in the separate bowl. Whisk it well. Preheat the air fryer to 365 F. Place the chicken cubes in the air fryer rack and sprinkle them with the olive oil. Cook the chicken for 15 minutes. When the chicken bites are cooked – chill them well. Enjoy!

Nutrition: calories 151, fat 8.5, fiber 0.4, carbs 1, protein 17

Air Fryer Meatballs

Prep time: 10 minutes
Cooking time: 13 minutes
Servings: 7

Ingredients:

- 1 egg
- 1-pound ground beef
- 1 tablespoon tomato puree
- 1 teaspoon salt
- 1 teaspoon curry paste
- ½ teaspoon ground coriander
- ½ white onion, grated
- 1 tablespoon butter
- ¼ teaspoon chili flakes

Directions:

Beat the egg in the bowl. Add the salt, curry paste, ground coriander, grated onion, and chili flakes. Mix the mixture up till the curry paste is dissolved. After this, add the ground beef and stir it carefully until homogenous. Then preheat the air fryer to 3660 F. Make 7 small meatballs from the ground beef mixture. Then place the meatballs in the air fryer basket tray. Add butter and tomato puree. Cook the meatballs for 13 minutes. Stir the meatballs after 7 minutes of cooking. When the meatballs are cooked – transfer them to the serving plate. Enjoy!

Nutrition: calories 153, fat 6.8, fiber 0.2, carbs 1.2, protein 20.6

Easy Cooked Chicken Wings

Prep time: 15 minutes
Cooking time: 12 minutes
Servings: 5

Ingredients:

- 1 teaspoon stevia extract
- 1 teaspoon salt
- 1-pound chicken wings
- 1 teaspoon paprika
- 1 teaspoon dried oregano
- 1 tablespoon olive oil

Directions:

Combine the salt, paprika, and dried oregano in the bowl and stir it. After this, sprinkle the chicken wings with the spice mixture. Then sprinkle the chicken wings with the stevia extract. Preheat the air fryer to 400 F. Place the prepared chicken wings in the air fryer rack and spray them with the olive oil. After this, cook the meat for 12 minutes. When the chicken wings are cooked – place them on the paper towel. Then serve. Taste it!

Nutrition: calories 199, fat 9.6, fiber 0.3, carbs 0.4, protein 26.3

Keto French Fries

Prep time: 10 minutes
Cooking time: 15 minutes
Servings: 6

Ingredients:
- 2 carrots
- 1 teaspoon paprika
- ¼ teaspoon ground white pepper
- ¼ teaspoon salt
- 1 tablespoon olive oil

Directions:
Peel the carrot and cut it into the strips. Cover the air fryer basket tray with the parchment and place the carrot strips there. Then sprinkle the carrot strips with the ground white pepper, paprika, and salt. Spray the carrot strips with the olive oil. Preheat the air fryer to 365 F. Cook the carrot fries for 15 minutes. The time can be less or more – depends on the size of the carrot strips. Then transfer the fries to the serving plate and chill them. Enjoy!

Nutrition: calories 30, fat 2.4, fiber 0.7, carbs 2.3, protein 0.2

Eggplant Bites with Parmesan

Prep time: 8 minutes
Cooking time: 14 minutes
Servings: 4

Ingredients:
- 1 eggplant
- ½ teaspoon turmeric
- ¼ teaspoon salt
- 4 oz. Parmesan, sliced
- 1 teaspoon olive oil

Directions:
Cut the eggplants into four bites. Then sprinkle the eggplant bites with the turmeric, salt, and stir them well. After this, preheat the air fryer to 400 F. Place the eggplants bites in the air fryer basket tray and spray them with the olive oil. After this, cook the eggplant bites for 13 minutes. Then cover the eggplant bites with the sliced Parmesan. Cook the dish for 1 minute more. Then transfer the eggplant bites on the serving plate and chill them till the cheese started to be solid. Serve and enjoy!

Nutrition: calories 131, fat 7.5, fiber 4.1, carbs 7.9, protein 10.3

Zucchini Chips

Prep time: 8 minutes
Cooking time: 13 minutes
Servings: 5

Ingredients:

- 2 zucchini
- 1 teaspoon olive oil
- ½ teaspoon salt
- 1 teaspoon paprika

Directions:

Wash the zucchini carefully and slice it into the chips pieces. Preheat the air fryer to 370 F. Sprinkle the zucchini slices with the salt and paprika. After this, place the zucchini slices in the air fryer rack. Sprinkle the zucchini slices with the olive oil gently. Cook the zucchini strips for 13 minutes. Turn the zucchini strips into another side during the cooking if desired. When the zucchini chips are cooked let them chill well. Serve the zucchini chips or keep them in the paper bag.

Nutrition: calories 22, fat 1.1, fiber 1, carbs 2.9, protein 1

Radish Chips

Prep time: 8 minutes
Cooking time: 15 minutes
Servings: 12

Ingredients:

- 1-pound radish
- 2 tablespoons olive oil
- 1 teaspoon salt

Directions:

Wash the radish carefully and slice it into the chips size. After this, sprinkle the radish chips with the salt. Spray the radish chips with the olive oil. Preheat the air fryer to 375 F. Place the radish slices in the air fryer rack and cook the chips for 15 minutes. When the radish chips get the desired texture – they are cooked. Chill the chips and serve them. Enjoy!

Nutrition: calories 26, fat 2.4, fiber 0.6, carbs 1.3, protein 0.3

Avocado Fries

Prep time: 10 minutes
Cooking time: 10 minutes
Servings: 3

Ingredients:
- 1 avocado, pitted
- ½ teaspoon salt
- 1 teaspoon ground black pepper
- ½ teaspoon paprika
- 1 egg
- 1 tablespoon coconut flour
- 1 teaspoon olive oil

Directions:
Peel the avocado and cut it into the thick strips. Then beat the egg in the bowl and whisk it. Combine the salt, ground black pepper, paprika, and coconut flour. Sprinkle the avocado thick strips with the whisked egg. Then coat every avocado strip into the spice dry mixture. Place the avocado strips in the air fryer rack and spray them with the olive oil. Then set the air fryer to 390 F and cook the avocado fries for 10 minutes. After this, shake the avocado fries gently and cook them for 5 minutes more. When the avocado fries are cooked let them chill. Serve the dish!

Nutrition: calories 184, fat 16.4, fiber 5.8, carbs 8.2, protein 3.6

Keto-Jerk Chicken Wings

Prep time: 15 minutes
Cooking time: 14 minutes
Servings: 4

Ingredients:
- 1-pound chicken wings
- ½ teaspoon salt
- 1 teaspoon garlic powder
- ¼ teaspoon ground black pepper
- ¼ teaspoon cayenne pepper
- ½ teaspoon ground ginger
- 1 tablespoon mustard
- 1 tablespoon tomato puree

Directions:
Place the chicken wings in the mixing bowl. Sprinkle the chicken wings with the salt, garlic powder, ground black pepper, cayenne pepper, ground ginger, and mustard. Mix the chicken wings carefully. Then add the tomato puree and mix the chicken wings carefully again. Let the chicken wings for 10 minutes to marinate. Preheat the air fryer to 370 F. Place the chicken wings in the air fryer basket tray and cook the dish for 14 minutes. When the chicken wings are cooked – transfer them to the serving plate. Enjoy!

Nutrition: calories 234, fat 9.3, fiber 0.6, carbs 2.1, protein 33.7

Fried Shrimp Tails

Prep time: 10 minutes
Cooking time: 14 minutes
Servings: 6

Ingredients:
- 1-pound shrimp tails
- 1 tablespoon olive oil
- 1 teaspoon dried dill
- ½ teaspoon dried parsley
- 2 tablespoon coconut flour
- ½ cup heavy cream
- 1 teaspoon chili flakes

Directions:

Peel the shrimp tails and sprinkle them with the dried dill and dried parsley. Mix the shrimp tails carefully in the mixing bowl. After this, combine the coconut flour, heavy cream, and chili flakes in the separate bowl and whisk it until you get the smooth batter. Then preheat the air fryer to 330 F. Transfer the shrimp tails in the heavy crema batter and stir the seafood carefully. Then spray the air fryer rack and put the shrimp tails there. Cook the shrimp tails for 7 minutes. After this, turn the shrimp tails into another side. Cook the shrimp tails for 7 minutes more. When the seafood is cooked – chill it well. Enjoy!

Nutrition: calories 155, fat 7.6, fiber 1, carbs 3.2, protein 17.8

Calamari Rings

Prep time: 12 minutes
Cooking time: 8 minutes
Servings: 4

Ingredients:
- 1 cup almond flour
- 9 oz. calamari
- 1 egg
- ½ teaspoon lemon zest
- 1 teaspoon fresh lemon juice
- ½ teaspoon turmeric
- ¼ teaspoon salt
- ¼ teaspoon ground black pepper

Directions:

Wash and peel the calamari. Then slice the calamari into thick rings. Beat the egg in the bowl and whisk it. Sprinkle the whisked egg with the lemon zest, turmeric, salt, and ground black pepper. Sprinkle the calamari rings with the fresh lemon juice. After this, place the calamari rings in the whisked egg and stir it carefully. Leave the calamari rings in the egg mixture for 4 minutes. Then coat the calamari rings in the almond flour mixture well. Preheat the air fryer to 360 F. Transfer the calamari rings in the air fryer rack. Cook the calamari rings for 8 minutes. When the seafood snack is cooked – chill it. Serve and enjoy!

Nutrition: calories 190, fat 15.7, fiber 3.1, carbs 7, protein 8.7

Keto Meat Bombs

Prep time: 15 minutes
Cooking time: 14 minutes
Servings: 7

Ingredients:

- 6 oz. ground chicken
- 6 oz. ground beef
- 6 oz. ground pork
- ½ white onion, grated
- 3 garlic cloves, minced
- 1 tablespoon dried parsley
- ½ teaspoon salt
- ½ teaspoon chili flakes
- 1 egg
- 1 tablespoon butter

Directions:

Put the ground chicken, ground beef, and ground pork in the mixing bowl. Add the grated onion, minced garlic, dried parsley, salt, and chili flakes. Crack the egg into the bowl with the ground meat. Then stir the meat mixture with the help of the hands. Melt butter and add it to the ground meat mixture. Stir it. Leave the ground meat mixture for 5 minutes to rest. Preheat the air fryer to 370 F. Make the small meat bombs from the meat mixture and put them in the air fryer. Cook the meatballs for 14 minutes. Then let the cooked meatballs chill gently. Serve!

Nutrition: calories 155, fat 6.5, fiber 0.2, carbs 1.3, protein 21.8

Bacon Mozzarella Balls

Prep time: 10 minutes
Cooking time: 10 minutes
Servings: 6

Ingredients:

- 5 oz. bacon, sliced
- 10 oz. mozzarella
- ¼ teaspoon ground black pepper
- ¼ teaspoon paprika

Directions:

Sprinkle the sliced bacon with the ground black pepper and paprika. Then wrap the mozzarella balls in the sliced bacon. Secure the mozzarella balls with the toothpicks. Preheat the air fryer to 360 F. Put the mozzarella balls in the air fryer rack and cook for 10 minutes. When the balls are cooked – let them chill until the room temperature. Enjoy!

Nutrition: calories 262, fat 18.2, fiber 0.1, carbs 2.1, protein 22.1

Toasted Nuts

Prep time: 5 minutes
Cooking time: 9 minutes
Servings: 4

Ingredients:

- ¼ cup hazelnuts
- ¼ cup walnuts
- ½ cup pecans
- ½ cup macadamia nuts
- 1 tablespoon olive oil
- 1 teaspoon salt

Directions:

Preheat the air fryer to 320 F. Place the hazelnuts, walnuts, pecans, and macadamia nuts in the air fryer. Cook the nuts for 8 minutes. Stir the nuts after 4 minutes of the cooking. At the end of the cooking, sprinkle the nuts with the olive oil and salt and shake them well. Cook the nuts for 1 minute more. Then transfer the cooked nuts in the serving ramekins. Enjoy!

Nutrition: calories 230, fat 23.9, fiber 2.4, carbs 3.9, protein 3.9

Flax Seeds Wraps

Prep time: 10 minutes
Cooking time: 2 minutes
Servings: 2

Ingredients:

- 1 cucumber
- 1 egg
- 3 oz. flax seeds
- 3 oz. mozzarella, grated
- 1 tablespoon water
- ½ tablespoon butter
- ¼ teaspoon baking soda
- ¼ teaspoon salt

Directions:

Crack the egg into the bowl and whisk it. Sprinkle the whisked egg with the flax seeds, grated mozzarella, water, baking soda, and salt. Whisk the mixture. Preheat the air fryer to 360 F. Toss the butter in the air fryer basket and melt it. Separate the egg liquid into 2 servings. Pour the first part of the serving in the air fryer basket. Cook it for 1 minute from the one side. After this, turn the "pancake" to another side and cook for 1 minute more. Repeat the same steps with the remaining egg mixture. Then cut the cucumber into the cubes. Separate the cubed cucumber into 2 parts. Place the cucumber cubes in the center of every egg pancake. Wrap the egg pancakes. Enjoy!

Nutrition: calories 424, fat 26.1, fiber 12.3, carbs 19.3, protein 23.7

Zucchini Fritters with Dill and Hard Cheese

Prep time: 10 minutes
Cooking time: 8 minutes
Servings: 7

Ingredients:
- 4 oz. Mozzarella
- 3 oz. Cheddar cheese
- 1 zucchini, grated
- 2 tablespoon dried dill
- 1 tablespoon coconut flour
- 1 tablespoon almond flour
- ¼ teaspoon salt
- 1 teaspoon butter

Directions:
Shred Cheddar cheese, and Mozzarella cheese. Combine the grated zucchini with the shredded cheese. Add dried dill and coconut flour. After this, add almond flour and salt. Stir the zucchini mass carefully with the help of the fork. When the mass is homogenous – let it for 3 minutes. Preheat the air fryer to 400 F. Melt the butter in the air fryer tray. Make the zucchini fritters from the zucchini mixture and put them in the melted butter. Cook the zucchini fritters for 5 minutes. After this, turn the zucchini fritters to another side and cook them for 3 minutes more. Serve the cooked zucchini fritters and enjoy!

Nutrition: calories 133, fat 9.6, fiber 1.3, carbs 3.7, protein 9.1

Keto Sesame Cloud Buns

Prep time: 15 minutes
Cooking time: 13 minutes
Servings: 10

Ingredients:
- 1 cup almond flour
- 5 tablespoon sesame seeds
- 1 tablespoon pumpkin seeds, crushed
- 1 teaspoon stevia extract
- ½ tablespoon baking powder
- 1 teaspoon apple cider vinegar
- ¼ teaspoon salt
- ½ cup water, hot
- 4 eggs

Directions:
Combine the dry ingredients: place the almond flour, sesame seeds, crushed pumpkin seeds, baking powder, and salt in the big mixing bowl. Then beat the eggs in the separate bowl. Whisk them and add stevia extract and apple cider vinegar. Stir the egg mixture gently. Then pour the hot water in the dried mixture. Stir it little and add the whisked egg mixture. Knead the homogenous non-sticky dough. Preheat the air fryer to 350 F. Cover the air fryer basket with the parchment. Make 10 small buns from the dough and put them in the air fryer. Cook the sesame cloud buns for 13 minutes. Then check if the buns are cooked. If the buns need little bit more time – cook them for 1 minute more. Then let the cooked buns chill little. Remove them from the air fryer and serve. Enjoy!

Nutrition: calories 72, fat 5.8, fiber 0.9, carbs 2.3, protein 3.8

Avocado Stick in Bacon Wraps

Prep time: 15 minutes
Cooking time: 11 minutes
Servings: 8

Ingredients:
- 2 avocado, pitted
- 1 egg
- 1 tablespoon coconut flakes
- ½ teaspoon salt
- 1 teaspoon paprika
- 1 teaspoon turmeric
- ½ teaspoon ground black pepper
- 1 teaspoon olive oil
- 5 oz. bacon, sliced
- 1 teaspoon dried rosemary

Directions:
Peel the avocados and cut them into the medium strips. Beat the egg in the bowl and whisk it. Sprinkle the whisked egg with the coconut flakes, salt, paprika, turmeric, ground black pepper, and dried rosemary. Put the avocado strips in the egg mixture. Then wrap the avocado sticks in the sliced bacon. Preheat the air fryer to 360 F. Place the wrapped avocado sticks in the air fryer rack. Cook the dish for 6 minutes on one side. After this, turn the avocado sticks into another side. Cook the dish for 5 minutes more. Then let the cooked dish chill little. Serve it and enjoy!

Nutrition: calories 216, fat 18.6, fiber 3.7, carbs 5.2, protein 8.3

Keto Crab Cakes

Prep time: 15 minutes
Cooking time: 10 minutes
Servings: 6

Ingredients:
- 12 oz crabmeat
- ¼ teaspoon salt
- 1 teaspoon chili powder
- 1 teaspoon ground white pepper
- 1 egg
- 1 tablespoon almond flour
- 1 tablespoon butter
- 1 tablespoon chives

Directions:
Chop the crab meat into the tiny pieces. Put the chopped crabmeat in the bowl. Sprinkle the crabmeat with the salt, chili powder, ground white pepper, and chives. Stir the mixture gently with the help of the spoon. Then beat the egg in the crabmeat. Add almond flour and stir it carefully. When you get the smooth texture of the seafood – the mixture is done. Preheat the air fryer to 400 F. Take 2 spoons and place the small amount of the crabmeat mixture in one of them. Cover it with the second spoon and make the crab cake. Toss the butter in the air fryer and melt it. Transfer the crab cakes in the air fryer and cook them for 10 minutes. Turn the crab cakes into another side after 5 minutes of cooking. When the dish is cooked – chill them gently. Enjoy!

Nutrition: calories 107, fat 6.1, fiber 0.8, carbs 2.6, protein 9.1

Hot Jalapeno Bites

Prep time: 15 minutes
Cooking time: 11 minutes
Servings: 5

Ingredients:
- 6 oz. bacon, sliced
- 1 cup jalapeno pepper
- ½ teaspoon salt
- ½ teaspoon paprika
- 1 teaspoon olive oil

Directions:
Wash the jalapeno peppers carefully. Combine the salt, paprika, and olive oil together. Stir it carefully. Brush the jalapeno peppers with the olive oil mixture generously. Then wrap every jalapeno pepper in the bacon slices. Secure the jalapeno bites with the toothpicks. Preheat the air fryer to 360 F. Put the jalapeno bites in the air fryer rack. Cook the jalapeno bites for 11 minutes. The bacon should be a little bit crunchy. Then transfer the cooked jalapeno pepper bites on the plate and cover them with the paper towel to get rid of the bacon fat. Serve and taste it!

Nutrition: calories 198, fat 15.3, fiber 0.6, carbs 1.7, protein 12.9

Keto Nuggets

Prep time: 15 minutes
Cooking time: 10 minutes
Servings: 5

Ingredients:
- 1-pound chicken fillet
- ½ teaspoon salt
- ½ teaspoon ground black pepper
- ½ teaspoon chili pepper
- 2 eggs
- ½ cup coconut flour

Directions:
Cut the chicken fillet into the nugget size pieces. Crack the eggs into the bowl and whisk them. Combine the coconut flour, chili pepper, salt, and ground black pepper in the big mixing bowl. Shake it well to make the homogenous mixture. Dip the nuggets in the whisked egg. Then coat the chicken nuggets in the almond flour mixture. Preheat the air fryer to 360 F. Transfer the coated chicken nuggets in the air fryer rack and cook them for 10 minutes. When the snack is cooked – serve it immediately. Enjoy!

Nutrition: calories 246, fat 9.7, fiber 4.9, carbs 8.3, protein 30.1

Moroccan Lamb Balls

Prep time: 15 minutes
Cooking time: 14 minutes
Servings: 6

Ingredients:

- 1 teaspoon cumin seeds
- 1 teaspoon coriander seeds
- 1 garlic clove, sliced
- 12 oz. ground lamb
- 2 tablespoon fresh lemon juice
- 1 egg
- 1 teaspoon dried mint
- 2 tablespoon heavy cream

Directions:

Combine the ground lamb and sliced garlic in the bowl. Sprinkle the meat mixture with the coriander seeds and cumin seeds. Then sprinkle the ground lamb with the fresh lemon juice and dried mint. Stir the ground lamb mixture with the help of the fork. Beat the egg in the forcemeat mixture. Stir it. Preheat the air fryer 360 F. Make the meatballs from the lamb mixture and place them in the air fryer. Cook the lamb balls for 8 minutes. Then sprinkle the lamb balls with the heavy cream and cook the dish for 6 minutes more. Then place the cocktail stick in every lamb balls and serve them. Enjoy!

Nutrition: calories 137, fat 6.9, fiber 0.1, carbs 0.7, protein 17.1

Lamb Burgers

Prep time: 15 minutes
Cooking time: 9 minutes
Servings: 6

Ingredients:

- 1-pound ground lamb
- 1 white onion, grated
- 1 teaspoon minced garlic
- 1 teaspoon salt
- ½ teaspoon chili pepper
- 1 teaspoon ground black pepper
- 1 large egg
- 2 tablespoon coconut flour
- 1 teaspoon olive oil

Directions:

Combine the ground lamb with the grated onion. Stir it carefully and sprinkle the mixture with minced garlic and salt. Add chili pepper, ground black pepper, and coconut flour. Then beat the egg into the mixture and mix it up with the help of the fingertips. Place the ground lamb mixture in the fridge for 10 minutes. Meanwhile, preheat the air fryer to 400 F. Make the balls from the ground lamb mixture and flatten them to make the shape of the burgers. Place the lamb burgers in the air fryer rack and sprinkle them with the olive oil. Cook the lamb burgers for 6 minutes. Then turn them into another side with the help of the spatula. Cook the lamb burgers for 3 minutes more. Serve the lamb burgers only hot. Enjoy!

Nutrition: calories 178, fat 7.4, fiber 1.5, carbs 3.9, protein 22.9

Stuffed Mushroom Hats

Prep time: 10 minutes
Cooking time: 5 minutes
Servings: 7

Ingredients:

- 9 oz. mushroom hats
- 6 oz. Cheddar cheese, shredded
- 1 teaspoon dried dill
- 1 teaspoon dried parsley
- ½ teaspoon salt
- 1 tablespoon butter

Directions:

Remove the flesh from the mushroom hats and grind it. Combine the ground mushroom flesh with the dried dill and dried parsley. Add salt and butter and mix it. It is better to take the soft butter – the procedure of the mixing will be easier. Then combine the mixed mixture with the shredded cheese. Stir it. Fill the mushroom hats with the cheese mixture. Preheat the air fryer to 400 F. Put the mushroom hats in the air fryer rack and cook them for 5 minutes. Transfer the cooked mushroom hats in the serving plate. Enjoy!

Nutrition: calories 121, fat 9.8, fiber 0.4, carbs 1.6, protein 7.3

Turnip Slices

Prep time: 12 minutes
Cooking time: 10 minutes
Servings: 8

Ingredients:

- 1 teaspoon garlic powder
- 1-pound turnip
- 1 teaspoon salt
- 3 oz. Parmesan, shredded
- 1 tablespoon olive oil

Directions:

Peel the turnip and slice it. Sprinkle the sliced turnip with the salt and garlic powder. Then sprinkle the turnip slices with the olive oil. Preheat the air fryer to 360 F. Put the turnip slices in the air fryer basket and cook them for 10 minutes. When the snack is cooked – transfer it to the serving plates and chill well. Enjoy!

Nutrition: calories 66, fat 4.1, fiber 1.1, carbs 4.3, protein 4

Cucumber Chips

Prep time: 10 minutes
Cooking time: 11 minutes
Servings: 12

Ingredients:

- 1-pound cucumber
- 1 teaspoon salt
- 1 tablespoon smoked paprika
- ½ teaspoon garlic powder

Directions:

Wash the cucumbers carefully and slice them in the shape of chips. Sprinkle the sliced cucumber chips with the salt, smoked paprika, and garlic powder. Preheat the air fryer to 370 F. Place the cucumber slices in the air fryer rack. Cook the cucumber chips for 11 minutes. Then transfer the cucumber chips in the paper towel and chill them well. Serve the cucumber chips immediately or keep them in the paper bag. Enjoy!

Nutrition: calories 8, fat 0.1, fiber 0.4, carbs 1.8, protein 0.4

Spinach Balls with Garlic

Prep time: 15 minutes
Cooking time: 11 minutes
Servings: 7

Ingredients:

- 4 large eggs
- 1 cup spinach
- ½ teaspoon salt
- 1 tablespoon minced garlic
- 8 oz. ground chicken
- 2 tablespoon almond flour
- 1 teaspoon olive oil
- 1 teaspoon smoked paprika
- 1 teaspoon coconut flour

Directions:

Beat the eggs and transfer them to the blender. Add the cup of the spinach, salt, minced garlic, almond flour, smoked paprika, and coconut flour. Blend it well until you get the texture of the forcemeat. Then transfer the prepared mixture into the bowl. Add the ground chicken and stir it. Make the palms wet and make the medium balls from the spinach mixture. Preheat the air fryer to 370 F. Spray the air fryer basket with the olive oil inside. Put the spinach balls in the air fryer and cook them for 11 minutes. When the spinach balls are cooked – they will have a tender taste. Let them chill until the room temperature. Serve the snack immediately or keep it in the plastic vessel in the fridge. Enjoy!

Nutrition: calories 159, fat 10, fiber 1.2, carbs 2.9, protein 15

Eggplants Chips

Prep time: 15 minutes
Cooking time: 13 minutes
Servings: 10

Ingredients:

- 1 teaspoon onion powder
- 1 teaspoon salt
- 3 eggplants
- 1 teaspoon paprika
- ½ teaspoon ground black pepper
- 1 tablespoon canola oil

Directions:

Wash the eggplants and slice them into the chips pieces. Sprinkle the eggplant slices with the salt and let them make the eggplant let juice and bitterness. Then dry the eggplant slices and sprinkle them with the onion powder, paprika, and ground black pepper. Stir the eggplant slices with the help of the fingertips. Then preheat the air fryer to 400 F. Place the eggplant slices in the air fryer rack and cook them for 13 minutes. The temperature of cooking depends on the thickness of the eggplant slices. When the chips are cooked – cool them. Enjoy!

Nutrition: calories 55, fat 1.7, fiber 5.9, carbs 10.1, protein 1.7

Broccoli Crisps

Prep time: 15 minutes
Cooking time: 13 minutes
Servings: 6

Ingredients:

- 3 tablespoon heavy cream
- 1 tablespoon almond flour
- ½ teaspoon salt
- ½ teaspoon turmeric
- 1 teaspoon ground black pepper
- 1-pound broccoli

Directions:

Wash the broccoli and separate it into the small florets. Then combine the almond flour, salt, turmeric, and ground black pepper in the shallow spice bowl. Shake it well to get the homogenous spice mixture. Sprinkle the small broccoli florets with the spice mixture. Stir it carefully. Then sprinkle the broccoli florets with the heavy cream and mix them up. Sprinkle the broccoli florets with the remaining spices one more time. Preheat the air fryer to 360 F. Put the prepared broccoli florets in the air fryer rack. Cook the broccoli florets for 10 minutes. After this, shake the broccoli carefully. Cook the broccoli crisps for 3 minutes more. Let the cooked broccoli crisps chill gently. Serve the dish!

Nutrition: calories 80, fat 5.4, fiber 2.6, carbs 6.6, protein 3.3

Spicy Kale Chips

Prep time: 10 minutes
Cooking time: 8 minutes
Servings: 14

Ingredients:
- 1-pound kale
- 1 teaspoon salt
- 1 teaspoon chili pepper
- 2 teaspoon canola oil

Directions:

Wash the kale and dry it well. Then tear the kale roughly. Preheat the air fryer to 370 F. Sprinkle the kale with the salt, chili pepper, and canola oil. Mix it up. Place the kale on the air fryer rack and cook for 5 minutes. After this, shake the kale and cook it for 3 minutes more. Chill the cooked kale chips and keep them in the dry place. Taste it!

Nutrition: calories 22, fat 0.7, fiber 0.5, carbs 3.4, protein 1

Kohlrabi Chips

Prep time: 7 minutes
Cooking time: 20 minutes
Servings: 10

Ingredients:
- 1-pound kohlrabi
- 1 teaspoon salt
- 1 tablespoon sesame oil
- 1 teaspoon smoked paprika

Directions:

Peel the kohlrabi. Slice it into the thin pieces. Sprinkle the kohlrabi slices with the salt, smoked paprika, and sesame oil. Shake the mixture. Preheat the air fryer to 320 F. Put the kohlrabi slices in the air fryer rack and cook for 20 minutes. You can stir the kohlrabi chips during cooking. Then chill the kohlrabi chips well. Serve and taste!

Nutrition: calories 25, fat 1.4, fiber 1.7, carbs 2.9, protein 0.8

Kohlrabi French Fries

Prep time: 10 minutes
Cooking time: 20 minutes
Servings: 8

Ingredients:

- 1 egg
- 2 tablespoon almond flour
- ½ teaspoon salt
- 1 teaspoon ground black pepper
- 1 teaspoon thyme
- 1 tablespoon olive oil
- 14 oz. kohlrabi

Directions:

Crack the egg and whisk it. Sprinkle the whisked egg with the salt, ground black pepper, and thyme. Whisk it for 1 minute. Peel the kohlrabi and cut it into pieces for French fries. Then put the kohlrabi pieces in the whisked egg mixture. After this, coat the kohlrabi in the almond flour. Preheat the air fryer to 360 F. Spray the kohlrabi with the olive oil and put in the air fryer. Cook the kohlrabi French fries for 20 minutes. Stir the kohlrabi fries frequently. When the kohlrabi French fries are cooked – chill them until warm. Enjoy!

Nutrition: calories 77, fat 5.9, fiber 2.7, carbs 4.9, protein 3.1

Rutabaga Fries

Prep time: 10 minutes
Cooking time: 18 minutes
Servings: 8

Ingredients:

- 1-pound rutabaga
- 1 teaspoon garlic powder
- 2 teaspoon sesame oil
- ½ teaspoon salt
- ½ teaspoon chili pepper

Directions:

Cut the rutabaga into the strips and sprinkle it with the garlic powder, sesame oil, salt, and chili pepper. Massage the rutabaga slices with the help of the fingertips. Then preheat the air fryer to 365 F. Place the rutabaga fries in the air fryer and cook them for 18 minutes. Stir the snack frequently. When the rutabaga fries are cooked – let them chill and serve. Enjoy!

Nutrition: calories 32, fat 1.2, fiber 1.5, carbs 4.9, protein 0.8

Daikon Chips

Prep time: 10 minutes
Cooking time: 15 minutes
Servings: 7

Ingredients:
- 1 teaspoon ground red pepper
- 3 teaspoon olive oil
- ½ teaspoon ground black pepper
- 1 teaspoon salt
- 15 oz. daikon

Directions:
Combine the ground red pepper, olive oil, ground black pepper, and salt in the small bowl. Whisk it. Then slice the daikon into the chips. Preheat the air fryer to 375 F. Brush daikon chips with the olive oil mixture. Place the daikon chips in the air fryer rack. Cook the chips for 16 minutes. Stir the daikon chips after 8 minutes of cooking. Then chill the chips and serve. Enjoy!

Nutrition: calories 30, fat 2, fiber 1.3, carbs 2.7, protein 1.3

Fried Pickles

Prep time: 10 minutes
Cooking time: 10 minutes
Servings: 7

Ingredients:
- 12 oz. pickles
- 2 eggs
- 1 teaspoon salt
- 1 teaspoon ground black pepper
- ½ cup almond flour
- 1 tablespoon olive oil

Directions:
Slice the pickles. Beat the eggs and whisk them. Combine the salt and ground black pepper. Stir the mixture. Put the sliced pickles in the whisked egg mixture. Then sprinkle the sliced pickles with the salt mixture. Dip the pickles into the egg mixture one more time. After this, coat the pickles in the almond flour. Preheat the air fryer to 400 F. Spray the air fryer with the olive oil inside. Place the sliced pickles there and cook for 10 minutes. Serve the cooked snack warm. Enjoy!

Nutrition: calories 53, fat 4.4, fiber 0.9, carbs 1.8, protein 2.2

Catfish Bites

Prep time: 12 minutes
Cooking time: 16 minutes
Servings: 6

Ingredients:

- 1-pound catfish fillet
- 1 teaspoon minced garlic
- 1 large egg
- ½ onion, diced
- 1 tablespoon butter, melted
- 1 teaspoon turmeric
- 1 teaspoon ground thyme
- 1 teaspoon ground coriander
- ¼ teaspoon ground nutmeg
- 1 teaspoon flax seeds

Directions:

Cut the catfish fillet into 6 bites. Sprinkle the fish bites with the minced garlic. Stir it. Then add diced onion, turmeric, ground thyme, ground coriander, ground nutmeg, and flax seeds. Mix the catfish bites gently. Preheat the air fryer to 360 F. Spray the catfish bites with the melted butter. Then freeze them. Put the catfish bites in the air fryer basket. Cook the catfish bites for 16 minutes. When the dish is cooked – chill it. Enjoy!

Nutrition: calories 140, fat 8.7, fiber 0.5, carbs 1.6, protein 13.1

French Artichoke Dip

Prep time: 15 minutes
Cooking time: 27 minutes
Servings: 7

Ingredients:

- 1 cup spinach
- 8 oz. artichoke, chopped
- ½ cup heavy cream
- 5 oz. Cheddar cheese
- ¼ teaspoon salt
- 1 teaspoon paprika
- ½ teaspoon ground coriander
- ½ cup cream cheese
- ½ teaspoon garlic powder
- 1 teaspoon olive oil

Directions:

Put the chopped artichoke in the foil. Sprinkle it with the salt, paprika, garlic powder, and ground coriander. Sprinkle the artichokes with the olive oil. Wrap the artichoke in the foil. Preheat the air fryer to 360 F. Place the wrapped artichoke in the air fryer and cook it for 25 minutes. Meanwhile, chop the spinach roughly and place it in the blender. Add the heavy cream, salt, paprika, ground coriander, and cream cheese. Blend it until homogenous. When the time is over – remove the artichoke from the air fryer and add it to the spinach mixture. Blend it for 2 minutes. Pour the blended mixture into the air fryer. Add heavy cream. Shred Cheddar cheese and add it to the air fryer too. Stir it and cook for 3 minutes at 360 F. When the cheese is melted – the dip is cooked. Serve it warm.

Nutrition: calories 192, fat 16.4, fiber 2, carbs 4.8, protein 7.7

Herbed Tomatoes

Prep time: 8 minutes
Cooking time: 12 minutes
Servings: 2

Ingredients:

- 2 tomatoes
- ½ teaspoon salt
- 1 teaspoon ground white pepper
- ½ teaspoon thyme
- ½ teaspoon ground coriander
- ½ teaspoon cilantro
- ½ teaspoon dried oregano
- 1 tablespoon olive oil

Directions:

Cut the tomatoes into halves. Then remove the flash from the tomatoes. Sprinkle the prepared tomato halves with the salt, ground white pepper, thyme, ground coriander, cilantro, and dried oregano. Preheat the air fryer to 350 F. Spray the tomato halves with the olive oil. Then place them in the air fryer rack. Cook the tomatoes for 12 minutes. When the tomatoes are cooked – let them cool till they are warm. Serve!

Nutrition: calories 87, fat 7.3, fiber 2, carbs 5.9, protein 1.3

Pumpkin Fries

Prep time: 15 minutes
Cooking time: 15 minutes
Servings: 7

Ingredients:

- 1-pound pumpkin
- 1 teaspoon ground cinnamon
- ½ teaspoon ground ginger
- ½ teaspoon salt
- 1 teaspoon olive oil
- 1 teaspoon turmeric

Directions:

Peel the pumpkin and cut it into the thick strips. Sprinkle the pumpkin strips with the ground cinnamon, ground ginger, salt, and turmeric. Stir the pumpkin carefully and leave for 5 minutes to make it soaks all the spices. Preheat the air fryer to 360 F. Sprinkle the pumpkin with the olive oil and transfer it to the air fryer basket. Cook the pumpkin fries for 15 minutes. Stir the pumpkin fries during cooking 3 times. Then place the cooked pumpkin fries on the paper towel. Chill them for 3-4 minutes. Enjoy!

Nutrition: calories 30, fat 0.9, fiber 2.2, carbs 5.8, protein 0.8

Winter Squash Tots

Prep time: 15 minutes
Cooking time: 10 minutes
Servings: 5

Ingredients:

- 1 cup pumpkin puree
- 1 tablespoon almond flour
- ½ teaspoon ground nutmeg
- ¼ teaspoon salt
- ¼ cup coconut flour
- 1 teaspoon olive oil
- ¼ teaspoon turmeric

Directions:

Take the big bowl and combine the pumpkin puree, almond flour, ground nutmeg, salt, and turmeric. Mix the mixture with the help of the fork. Then add coconut flour. Mix it up again. The pumpkin mixture should be non-sticky. Separate the pumpkin dough into 5 parts and form 5 tots. Preheat the air fryer to 360 F. Spray the air fryer with the olive oil inside and cook the pumpkin tots for 10 minutes. When the dish is cooked - chill it. Taste it and enjoy!

Nutrition: calories 82, fat 4.6, fiber 4.5, carbs 9.3, protein 2.6

Bacon Shrimps

Prep time: 10 minutes
Cooking time: 10 minutes
Servings: 4

Ingredients:

- 8 oz. shrimp
- 5 oz. bacon, sliced
- 1 teaspoon fresh lemon juice
- ¼ teaspoon salt
- ¼ teaspoon turmeric
- ½ tablespoon canola oil
- ½ teaspoon dried rosemary

Directions:

Peel the shrimps and sprinkle them with the fresh lemon juice and salt. Mix the seafood with the help of the hands. Then sprinkle the shrimps with the turmeric and dried rosemary. Wrap the shrimps in the sliced bacon. Secure the shrimps with the toothpicks. Preheat the air fryer to 360 F. Spray the air fryer with the canola oil inside. Put the shrimps in the air fryer and cook them for 5 minutes from the each side. After this, let the shrimps chill little. Enjoy!

Nutrition: calories 276, fat 17.6, fiber 0.1, carbs 1.6, protein 26.1

Onion Squares

Prep time: 15 minutes
Cooking time: 8 minutes
Servings: 8

Ingredients:
- 2 white onions
- 1 cup almond flour
- 1 teaspoon baking powder
- ¼ tablespoon salt
- 1 cup heavy cream
- 1 teaspoon paprika
- 1 teaspoon sesame oil

Directions:

Peel the white onions and cut them into the medium squares. Then combine the almond flour, baking powder, salt, and paprika in the big bowl. Stir the dried mixture with the help of the fork. Then put the onion squares in the heavy cream and coat them well. After this, sprinkle the onion squares with the dried spice mixture from the each side. Sprinkle the onion squares with the sesame oil. Preheat the air fryer to 360 F. Put the onion squares in the air fryer and cook for 8 minutes. When the snack is cooked – serve it. Enjoy!

Nutrition: calories 89, fat 7.9, fiber 1.1, carbs 4.2, protein 1.4

Parmesan Green Beans

Prep time: 12 minutes
Cooking time: 5 minutes
Servings: 7

Ingredients:
- 14 oz. green beans
- 5 oz. Parmesan, shredded
- 1 egg
- 2 tablespoon coconut flakes
- 1 teaspoon dried oregano
- ½ teaspoon ground paprika
- 1 teaspoon butter

Directions:

Wash the green beans. Beat the egg in the bowl and whisk it. Preheat the air fryer to 400 F. Place the green beans in the whisked egg. After this, sprinkle the green beans with the coconut flakes, dried oregano, and ground paprika. Then add the shredded cheese and stir it carefully. Put the butter in the air fryer basket and melt it. Then add the green beans. Cook the dish for 5 minutes. The surface of the green beans can be a little bit crunchy. Stir the green beans and separate it into 7 servings. Enjoy!

Nutrition: calories 103, fat 6.1, fiber 2.2, carbs 5.3, protein 8.4

Fish Fries

Prep time: 10 minutes
Cooking time: 6 minutes
Servings: 6

Ingredients:

- 1-pound cod fillet
- 2 large eggs
- 1 tablespoon coconut oil
- ½ teaspoon salt
- 1 teaspoon ground black pepper
- 1 teaspoon turmeric
- 1 teaspoon paprika

Directions:

Cut the cod fillet into 6 parts (fries size). Beat the egg in the bowl and whisk it. Add the salt, ground black pepper, turmeric, and paprika. Stir it. Then dip the cod fillets in the egg mixture. Preheat the air fryer to 360 F. Spray the cod fillets with the coconut oil and put them in the air fryer rack. Cook the dish for 6 minutes. Stir the cod fries after 4 minutes of cooking. Remove the cooked fish fries from the air fryer. Serve the dish with the keto sauce. Enjoy!

Nutrition: calories 107, fat 4.7, fiber 0.3, carbs 0.8, protein 15.7

Wrapped Brussel Sprouts

Prep time: 15 minutes
Cooking time: 12 minutes
Servings: 6

Ingredients:

- 6 oz. bacon, sliced
- 16 oz. Brussel sprouts
- ½ teaspoon salt
- 2 teaspoon coconut flakes
- ¼ teaspoon ground red pepper
- 1 teaspoon apple cider vinegar
- 1 tablespoon olive oil

Directions:

Wash Brussel sprouts. Sprinkle the sliced bacon with the salt, coconut flakes, and ground red pepper. Sprinkle Brussel sprouts with the apple cider vinegar and olive oil. Then wrap Brussel sprouts in the sliced bacon. Secure Brussel sprouts with the toothpicks if desired. Preheat the air fryer to 365 F. Put wrapped Brussel sprouts in the air fryer and cook for 12 minutes. When the dish is cooked – the bacon should be a little bit crunchy. Enjoy!

Nutrition: calories 208, fat 14.6, fiber 2.9, carbs 7.4, protein 13.1

Desserts

Peanut Butter Cookies

Prep time: 15 minutes
Cooking time: 10 minutes
Servings: 8

Ingredients:

- 4 tablespoon Erythritol
- 8 tablespoon peanut butter
- 1 egg
- ¼ teaspoon salt

Directions:

Take the big bowl and put Erythritol there. Add peanut butter and salt. After this, crack the egg into the bowl with the peanut butter mixture. Mix up the dough until it is smooth and homogenous. After this, roll the dough with the help of the rolling pin. Make the rounds with the help of the cutter. Then make the cross with the help of the fork in every cookie. Preheat an air fryer to 360 F. Put the cookies in the air fryer basket. Cook the cookies for 10 minutes. When the cookies are cooked – let them chill well. Serve the cookies immediately or keep them in the closed glass jar. Enjoy!

Nutrition: calories 102, fat 8.6, fiber 1, carbs 10.7, protein 4.7

Chia Seeds Crackers

Prep time: 15 minutes
Cooking time: 4 minutes
Servings: 8

Ingredients:

- 5 tablespoons chia seeds
- 2 oz. Cheddar cheese, shredded
- ½ cup water
- 1 oz. psyllium husk powder
- 1 teaspoon olive oil
- 1 teaspoon onion powder
- 1 teaspoon paprika
- ½ teaspoon dried rosemary
- ½ teaspoon ground ginger

Directions:

Combine the chia seeds with water, husk powder, and onion powder. Add paprika, dried rosemary, and ground ginger. Shred Cheddar cheese and add it to the chia seed mixture. Mix the mixture and make the smooth dough. The dough should be very elastic. Then roll the dough and make the medium crackers with the help of the cutter. The crackers should be thin. Preheat the air fryer to 360 F. Put the chia seeds crackers in the air fryer tray. Cook the crackers for 4 minutes. Then chill the crackers and serve. Taste the crackers!

Nutrition: calories 109, fat 6.8, fiber 7.2, carbs 9, protein 3.9

Flax Seed Crackers

Prep time: 20 minutes
Cooking time: 5 minutes
Servings: 6

Ingredients:

- 1 egg
- 8 tablespoon coconut flour
- 1 tablespoon coconut flakes
- ½ teaspoon baking soda
- 1 teaspoon apple cider vinegar
- 2 tablespoon swerve
- 3 oz. hot water
- 5 tablespoon flax seeds
- ¼ teaspoon salt
- 1 teaspoon ground cinnamon
- 1 tablespoon olive oil

Directions:

Put the flax seeds in the blender and blend them to get the texture of the dough flour. Then combine the flax seeds with the coconut flour, coconut flakes, salt, and ground cinnamon. Combine the baking soda and apple cider vinegar in the spoon and stir it. Add the baking soda mixture in the flax seed mixture. Stir it carefully. Add hot water and olive oil. Whisk it gently and add swerve. Then crack the egg into the bowl and stir it until the mixture starts to be a little bit homogenous. After this, knead the cracker dough with the help of the fingertips. Add more almond flour if the dough sticks to hands. Then roll the cracker dough with the help of the rolling pin. Cut the dough into the medium crackers. Preheat the air fryer to 365 F. Put the crackers in the air fryer basket and cook for 5 minutes. Shake the crackers during the cooking to protect them from overcooking. Let the cooked crackers chill well. Serve!

Nutrition: calories 105, fat 6.2, fiber 5.9, carbs 8.8, protein 3.4

Sweet Fat Bombs

Prep time: 25 minutes
Cooking time: 7 minutes
Servings: 12

Ingredients:

- 5 tablespoon swerve
- 6 tablespoon peanut butter
- ½ teaspoon vanilla extract
- ¼ teaspoon salt
- 6 tablespoon Erythritol
- 1 teaspoon stevia extract
- 8 tablespoon fresh lemon juice
- 3 eggs
- 1 teaspoon lime zest
- 2 tablespoon coconut oil

Directions:

Melt the peanut butter and combine it with the swerve. Then add vanilla extract, salt, and Erythritol. Whisk the mixture. Take the truffle forms and place the peanut butter mixture there. Freeze the peanut mixture. Preheat the air fryer to 350 F. Combine the stevia extract, fresh lemon juice, lime zest, and coconut oil in the bowl. Whisk it well. After this, pour the fresh lemon mixture in the air fryer basket and cook it for 5 minutes. Stir it every 2 minutes. After this, crack the eggs in the lemon mixture and mix it up with the help of the hand mixer. When the curd mixture is smooth – cook it at 365 F for 2 minutes more. Then remove the cooked curd mixture and chill it well. Place the cooked curd mixture in the pastry bag. Remove the truffle from the freezer. Fill the truffles with the curd mixture and keep the bomb in the cold place. Enjoy!

Nutrition: calories 231, fat 24.3, fiber 0.5, carbs 10.3, protein 3.5

Poppy Seeds Balls

Prep time: 20 minutes
Cooking time: 8 minutes
Servings: 11

Ingredients:

- ½ cup heavy cream
- 1 cup coconut flour
- ¼ teaspoon salt
- ½ teaspoon ground cinnamon
- 4 tablespoon poppy seeds
- ¼ teaspoon ground ginger
- 1 teaspoon butter
- ½ teaspoon baking powder
- ½ teaspoon apple cider vinegar
- 3 tablespoon stevia extract

Directions:

Mix the coconut flour, salt, ground cinnamon, poppy seeds, ground ginger, and baking powder together in the bowl. Melt the butter gently and add in the dried mixture. After this, add apple cider vinegar and stevia extract. Add the heavy cream and knead the soft but elastic dough. Make the log from the prepared dough and cut it into 11 balls. Then preheat the air fryer to 365 F. Put the poppy seeds balls in the air fryer basket. Cook the balls for 3 minutes. After this, shake them little and cook for 5 minutes more. Check if the balls are cooked with the help of the toothpick. The time of cooking of the balls can be changed with the size of the poppy balls. Chill the poppy balls and keep them in the paper bag or cover them with the towel. Enjoy!

Nutrition: calories 83, fat 4.9, fiber 4.8, carbs 8.4, protein 2.1

Keto Cheesecake

Prep time: 25 minutes
Cooking time: 16
Servings: 6

Ingredients:

- 6 tablespoon butter, soft
- ½ cup almonds, sliced
- 1 tablespoon stevia extract
- ½ teaspoon vanilla extract
- 1 cup cream cheese
- 2 tablespoon swerve
- 2 eggs
- ¼ teaspoon ground cinnamon
- 1 teaspoon lemon zest

Directions:

Combine the sliced almonds with butter, stevia extract, and vanilla extract. Mix the mixture up – the cheesecake crust is cooked. Cover the air fryer tray with the parchment. Spread the air fryer tray with the cheesecake almond crust well. Then combine swerve, ground cinnamon, lemon zest, and cream cheese. Crack the eggs and mix the mixture with the hand mixer. When the mass is soft and fluffy – it is cooked. Pour the cream cheese mixture over the almond crust. Preheat the air fryer to 310 F. Cook the cheesecake for 16 minutes. When the cheesecake is cooked – chill it for at least 2 hours. Then cut the cheesecake into pieces. Enjoy!

Nutrition: calories 307, fat 30.4, fiber 1.1, carbs 3.7, protein 6.6

Coconut Cookies

Prep time: 15 minutes
Cooking time: 10 minutes
Servings: 20

Ingredients:

- 1/3 cup coconut flour
- 1 tablespoon coconut flakes
- 3 tablespoon coconut milk
- 3 tablespoon butter
- ¼ teaspoon salt
- 2 eggs
- ¼ teaspoon ground ginger
- ¼ teaspoon ground cinnamon
- 2 teaspoon stevia extract
- ½ teaspoon vanilla extract

Directions:

Sift the coconut flour and put it in the bowl. Add coconut flakes, salt, ground ginger, ground cinnamon, and vanilla extract. After this, add stevia extract. Crack the eggs into the separate bowl and whisk them with the help of the hand whisker. Then pour the whisked egg mixture in the coconut flour. Add butter and coconut milk. Mix it up with the help of the fork. When the cookie's dough is ready – make the medium balls from it. Flatten it gently. Preheat the air fryer to 365 F. Cover the air fryer tray with the parchment and place the coconut flatten balls there. Cook the cookies for 10 minutes. When the cookies are cooked – they will have light brown edges. Chill the cookies and serve!

Nutrition: calories 36, fat 3, fiber 0.9, carbs 1.6, protein 0.9

Pecan Bars

Prep time: 18 minutes
Cooking time: 23 minutes
Servings: 8

Ingredients:

- 1 cup almond flour
- ¼ cup hot water
- ¼ teaspoon salt
- 3 tablespoon stevia extract
- 1 teaspoon vanilla extract
- 2 tablespoon butter
- 4 tablespoon pecans, crushed
- ½ teaspoon baking powder
- ½ teaspoon apple cider vinegar
- ½ teaspoon sesame oil

Directions:

Preheat the butter until it is soft but not liquid. After this, combine the soft butter and almond flour. Then add salt, stevia extract, vanilla extract, water, baking powder, and apple cider vinegar. Sprinkle the almond flour mixture with sesame oil and knead the homogenous dough. Then add the crushed pecans and knead the dough for 2 minutes more. Preheat the air fryer to 350 F. Cover the air fryer tray with the parchment and place the almond flour dough there. Flatten it to make the flat surface. Cover it with the parchment and cook for 20 minutes. After this, remove the covering and cook the dish for 3 minutes more. When the time is over – chill the pecan dish and cut it into 8 bars. Serve it!

Nutrition: calories 157, fat 14.3, fiber 2.2, carbs 4.1, protein 3.7

Macadamia Nuts Brownies

Prep time: 15 minutes
Cooking time: 25 minutes
Servings: 12

Ingredients:

- 2 eggs
- 1/3 cup macadamia nuts, crushed
- 3 tablespoon butter, melted
- 1 cup coconut flour
- ½ teaspoon baking powder
- 1 teaspoon fresh lemon juice
- 4 oz. dark chocolate, melted
- 3 tablespoon swerve

Directions:

Beat the eggs in the mixer bowl and mix them. Add melted butter and keep mixing the mixture for 2 minutes more. After this, add coconut flour, baking powder, fresh lemon juice, melted dark chocolate, and swerve. Mix it up with the help of the silicon spatula. After this, add the crushed macadamia nuts and stir it carefully. Then preheat the air fryer to 355 F. Pour the brownie dough in the air fryer basket tray and cook it for 25 minutes. Cooked brownies should be soft but well cooked. Slice the brownies into 12 pieces. Enjoy!

Nutrition: calories 155, fat 10.2, fiber 4.6, carbs 13.5, protein 3.3

Coconut-Sunflower Bars

Prep time: 15 minutes
Cooking time: 16 minutes
Servings: 8

Ingredients:

- 2 tablespoon sunflower seeds
- 1 tablespoon coconut flakes
- ½ cup almond flour
- 2 tablespoon coconut milk
- 2 tablespoon butter
- ¼ teaspoon salt
- 2 tablespoon stevia extract
- 1 egg

Directions:

Crush the sunflower seeds and combine them with the coconut flakes. Then add the almond flour and salt. Stir the dried ingredients carefully. Beat the egg in the mixture. After this, add the coconut milk, butter, and stevia extract. Mix it up with the help of the spatula or use the hand mixer. Preheat the air fryer to 355 F. Pour the coconut mixture into the air fryer tray and cook it for 16 minutes. If the mixture is too thick – increase the time of cooking for 2-3 minutes more. Then chill the cooked mixture well. Cut it into 8 small bars. Enjoy!

Nutrition: calories 90, fat 8.2, fiber 1, carbs 2, protein 2.5

Green Avocado Pudding

Prep time: 10 minutes
Cooking time: 3minutes
Servings: 3

Ingredients:

- 1 tablespoon cocoa powder
- 1 avocado, pitted
- 3 teaspoon stevia extract
- ¼ teaspoon vanilla extract
- ¼ teaspoon salt
- 5 tablespoon almond milk

Directions:

Preheat the air fryer to 360 F. Peel the avocado and mash it with the help of the fork. Then combine it with the stevia extract, vanilla extract, salt, and almond milk. Then add the cocoa powder. Mix the mixture well with the help of the hand mixer. Then pour the pudding mixture into the air fryer basket. Cook it for 3 minutes. When the pudding is cooked – let it chill well. Serve it.

Nutrition: calories 199, fat 19.3, fiber 5.6, carbs 8.2, protein 2.2

Tender Sunflower Cookies

Prep time: 15 minutes
Cooking time: 10 minutes
Servings: 8

Ingredients:

- 5 oz. sunflower seed butter
- ½ teaspoon salt
- 1 tablespoon stevia extract
- 6 tablespoon coconut flour
- ¼ teaspoon salt
- ¼ teaspoon olive oil

Directions:

Combine the sunflower seed butter and coconut flour together. Sprinkle the mixture with salt and stevia extract. Add olive oil and mix it up. When you get the homogeneous texture of the dough – it is done. Separate the dough into 8 balls and flatten them gently. Preheat the air fryer to 365 F. Put the flattened balls in the air fryer rack. Cook the cookies for 10 minutes. When the cookies are cooked – let them cool well. Enjoy!

Nutrition: calories 126, fat 9.2, fiber 2.3, carbs 8.6, protein 4.2

Keto Chocolate Spread

Prep time: 10 minutes
Cooking time: 3 minutes
Servings: 6

Ingredients:
- 1 oz. dark chocolate
- 3 oz. hazelnuts, crushed
- 4 tablespoon butter
- ¼ cup almond milk
- ½ teaspoon vanilla extract
- 1 teaspoon stevia

Directions:
Preheat the air fryer to 360 F. Put the dark chocolate, crushed hazelnuts, butter, almond milk, vanilla extract, and stevia in the air fryer basket. Mix it up and cook for 2 minutes. Then mix the mixture with the help of the hand mixer. Cook the mixture for 1 minute. Then stir the mixture again and pour it into the glass vessel. Put the mixture in the fridge and let it cool until it is solid. Enjoy!

Nutrition: calories 206, fat 20.1, fiber 1.8, carbs 5.8, protein 2.8

Keto Vanilla Mousse

Prep time: 15 minutes
Cooking time: 6 minutes
Servings: 4

Ingredients:
- 1 teaspoon vanilla extract
- ½ cup cream cheese
- ½ cup almond milk
- ¼ cup blackberries
- 2 teaspoon stevia extract
- 2 tablespoon butter
- ¼ teaspoon cinnamon

Directions:
Preheat the air fryer to 320 F. Combine butter, vanilla extract, and almond milk and transfer the mixture in the air fryer. Cook the mixture for 6 minutes or until the almond milk mixture will be homogenous. Then stir it carefully and chill until the room temperature. Smash the blackberries. Whisk the cream cheese with the help of the hand whisker for 2 minutes. Add the smashed blackberries and whisk for 1 minute more. After this, add cinnamon and stevia extract. Stir it gently. Combine the almond-butter liquid and cream cheese mixture together. Mix it up with the help of the hand mixer. When the meal is homogenous – pour it into the glass vessel. Place it in the fridge and cool. Enjoy!

Nutrition: calories 228, fat 23.1, fiber 1.2, carbs 3.5, protein 3.1

Avocado Brownies

Prep time: 15 minutes
Cooking time: 20 minutes
Servings: 6

Ingredients:

- 1 avocado, pitted
- 2 teaspoon Erythritol
- ¼ teaspoon vanilla extract
- 1 oz. dark chocolate
- 3 tablespoon almond flour
- ½ teaspoon stevia powder
- 1 egg
- 1 teaspoon coconut oil
- ¼ teaspoon baking powder
- ¼ teaspoon salt

Directions:

Peel the avocado and chop it roughly. Put the chopped avocado in the blender. Melt the dark chocolate and add it to the blender too. After this, add vanilla extract and blend the mixture until it is smooth. Then add almond flour, stevia powder, coconut oil, baking powder, salt, and Erythritol. Beat the egg in the mixture and blend it until smooth. Preheat the air fryer to 355 F. Pour the avocado brownie mixture in the air fryer tray and flatten it with the help of the spatula. Cook the brownie dough for 20 minutes. When the meal is cooked – cut it into 6 brownie bars and chill. Enjoy!

Nutrition: calories 131, fat 11.2, fiber 2.8, carbs 8.3, protein 2.7

Chocolate Chips Cookies

Prep time: 15 minutes
Cooking time: 15 minutes
Servings: 5

Ingredients:

- 1 cup almond flour
- 3 tablespoon macadamia nuts, crushed
- 1 egg
- 3 tablespoon butter, unsalted
- 2 tablespoon dark chocolate chips
- ¼ teaspoon salt
- ¼ teaspoon baking powder
- ½ teaspoon vanilla extract
- 1 teaspoon stevia extract

Directions:

Beat the egg in the mixing bowl and whisk it with the help of the hand whisker. Add butter and almond flour. After this, add salt, baking powder, vanilla extract, and stevia extract. Sprinkle the mixture with the crushed macadamia nuts and dark chocolate chips. Knead the smooth dough. Then make 5 balls from the chocolate chips dough and flatten them little. Preheat the air fryer to 360 F. Put the cookies in the air fryer and cook them for 15 minutes. After this, let the cooked cookies chill little. Serve them!

Nutrition: calories 157, fat 15.2, fiber 1, carbs 4.2, protein 3

Cheesecake Mousse

Prep time: 20 minutes
Cooking time: 4 minutes
Servings: 6

Ingredients:

- ¼ cup heavy cream
- 1 egg
- ½ cup cream cheese
- 1/3 cup Erythritol
- ¼ teaspoon lime zest
- 2 scoop stevia

Directions:

Beat the egg in the mixer bowl and whisk it. Add the heavy cream and keep whisking it until the mixture is fluffy. Then add cream cheese, lime zest, stevia, and Erythritol. Whisk it well. Preheat the air fryer to 310 F. Pour the cheesecake mixture into the air fryer tray and cook it for 14 minutes. Stir it every 4 minutes. When the mousse is cooked – whisk it carefully with the help of the hand whisker. Chill the meal and enjoy!

Nutrition: calories 95, fat 9.3, fiber 0, carbs 14.1, protein 2.5

Sweet Bacon Cookies

Prep time: 10 minutes
Cooking time: 7 minutes
Servings: 6

Ingredients:

- 4 slices bacon, cooked, chopped
- 5 tablespoon peanut butter
- ¼ teaspoon baking soda
- 3 tablespoon swerve
- ½ teaspoon vanilla extract
- ¼ teaspoon ground ginger

Directions:

Take a big bowl and combine the baking soda, peanut butter, swerve, vanilla extract, and ground ginger together. Add chopped bacon and mix the dough up with the help of the spatula. When the dough is homogenous – make the log from it and cut it into 6 parts. Roll the balls from the dough and flatten them gently. Preheat the air fryer to 350 F. Place the cookies in the air fryer and cook for 7 minutes. When the cookies are cooked – let them chill well. Enjoy!

Nutrition: calories 109, fat 8.8, fiber 0.8, carbs 3.8, protein 5.2

Sunflower Seeds Pie

Prep time: 20 minutes
Cooking time: 20 minutes
Servings: 6

Ingredients:

- ½ cup sunflower seeds
- 1 cup almond flour
- ¼ cup heavy cream
- 2 eggs
- 1 teaspoon butter
- ½ teaspoon vanilla extract
- ½ teaspoon ground ginger
- 3 scoop stevia
- ½ teaspoon baking powder

Directions:

Beat the eggs in the big bowl and whisk them. Add heavy cream, butter, almond flour, vanilla extract, ground ginger, stevia, and baking powder. Mix the dough mixture gently with the help of the hand mixer. Then add the sunflower seeds and stir the dough with the help of the spatula. Leave the pie dough for 10 minutes to rest. Preheat the air fryer to 360 F. Transfer the dough to the air fryer dish and place it in the preheated air fryer. Cook the pie for 20 minutes. Then let the pie chill well. After this, discard it from the air fryer dish and cut into servings. Enjoy!

Nutrition: calories 180, fat 14.8, fiber 2.4, carbs 5.4, protein 6.8

Almond Sponge Cake

Prep time: 15 minutes
Cooking time: 18 minutes
Servings: 6

Ingredients:

- 5 eggs
- 1 cup almond flour
- ¼ teaspoon salt
- 3 scoop stevia

Directions:

Separate the egg whites and egg yolks and place them in the separate bowls. Then whisk the egg yolk for 3 minutes. Add the stevia and whisk it for 1 minute more. After this, whisk the egg whites until you get the strong peaks. Combine the whisked egg yolks with the almond flour and salt. Stir the mixture very slowly with the help of the spatula. After this, start to add the egg white peaks in the egg yolk mixture gradually. Stir it carefully until you get the fluffy yellow dough. Preheat the air fryer to 280 F. Pour the sponge cake dough in the air fryer tray and cook it for 18 minutes. Check if the sponge cake is cooked with the help of the toothpick. Chill the sponge cake carefully and discard it from the tray. Serve the sponge cake with the small amount of the blueberries. Enjoy!

Nutrition: calories 164, fat 12.5, fiber 2, carbs 4.3, protein 8.6

Blackberry Pie

Prep time: 15 minutes
Cooking time: 20 minutes
Servings: 8

Ingredients:

- 1 cup almond flour
- 2 tablespoon butter, unsalted
- 1 tablespoon baking powder
- 1 large egg
- ½ cup blackberries
- 1 scoop stevia extract

Directions:

Preheat the air fryer to 350 F. Beat the egg in the bowl and whisk it. Then add baking powder, stevia extract, and butter. Mix it up. Leave the 1 teaspoon almond flour. Put all the remaining almond flour in the egg mixture. Knead the smooth and non-sticky dough. Cover the air fryer tray with the parchment. Then put the dough in the air fryer dish and flatten it in the shape of the piecrust. Place the blackberries over the piecrust. Then sprinkle the pie with the 1 teaspoon of almond flour. Cook the pie for 20 minutes. When the surface of the pie is golden brown – it is cooked. Chill it well and slice into the serving. Enjoy!

Nutrition: calories 60, fat 3.5, fiber 0.9, carbs 2.5, protein 1.7

Coconut Pie

Prep time: 25 minutes
Cooking time: 10 minutes
Servings: 4

Ingredients:

- 1 cup almond flour
- 3 tablespoon butter
- ¼ teaspoon salt
- 1 scoop stevia
- 1 tablespoon ice water
- 3 eggs
- ½ cup heavy cream
- 1 teaspoon butter
- 2 tablespoon coconut flakes
- 1 teaspoon vanilla extract

Directions:

Preheat the air fryer to 360 F. Combine the almond flour and 3 tablespoons of the butter in the bowl. Add salt and stevia. Blend it well. When the mixture starts to be smooth – add ice water and blend it for 2 minutes more. Cover the air fryer crust with the parchment and place the dough there. Roll it with the help of the fingertips. Place the piecrust in the air fryer and cook for 7 minutes. Meanwhile, beat the eggs in the bowl and whisk them. Add the 1 teaspoon of butter and heavy cream and whisk it well for 3 minutes. Add coconut flakes and vanilla extract. Whisk it for 1 minute more. When the pie crust is cooked – remove it from the air fryer and chill it. Pour the whisked heavy cream mixture in the air fryer and cook it for 3 minutes at 365 F. Then whisk it carefully. Then pour the cooked heavy cream mixture over the piecrust. Chill it until the filling of the pie is a little bit solid. Serve it!

Nutrition: calories 190, fat 17.3, fiber 1.6, carbs 3.6, protein 5.3

Avocado Muffins

Prep time: 18 minutes
Cooking time: 12 minutes
Servings: 7

Ingredients:

- 1 oz. dark chocolate, melted
- 1 cup almond flour
- ½ cup avocado, pitted
- ½ teaspoon baking soda
- 4 tablespoon butter
- 1 teaspoon apple cider vinegar
- 3 scoop stevia powder
- 1 egg

Directions:

Put the almond flour in the bowl. Add baking soda and apple cider vinegar. After this, add melted chocolate and stevia powder. Crack the egg into the separate bowl and whisk it. Add whisked egg in the almond flour mixture. Add butter. Then peel the avocado and mash it. Add the mashed avocado in the almond flour mixture. Use the hand mixer to make the almond flour mixture smooth and homogenous. Preheat the air fryer to 355 F. Pour the almond flour mixture in the muffin forms. Fill ½ part of every muffin mold. Put the muffins in the air fryer and cook them for 9 minutes. Then reduce the temperature to 340 F and cook the muffins for 3 minutes more. Chill the cooked muffins and serve them! Enjoy!

Nutrition: calories 133, fat 12.4, fiber 1.3, carbs 4.2, protein 2.2

Cream Cheese Muffins

Prep time: 15 minutes
Cooking time: 10 minutes
Servings: 8

Ingredients:

- 1 eggs
- 1 cup cream cheese
- 1 cup almond flour
- ¼ teaspoon salt
- 1 teaspoon baking soda
- 1 teaspoon apple cider vinegar
- 2 teaspoon swerve
- 2 tablespoon coconut flakes

Directions:

Beat the egg in the bowl and add cream cheese. Whisk the mixture well. Sprinkle the cream cheese mixture with the almond flour, salt, baking soda, and apple cider vinegar. Add swerve and coconut flakes. Use the hand mixer to make the sour cream-like dough. Preheat the air fryer to 360 F. Fill the ½ part of every muffin mold with the muffin dough and put the muffins in the air fryer. Cook the muffins for 10 minutes. When the muffins are cooked – let them chill well. Then serve. Taste it!

Nutrition: calories 135, fat 12.8, fiber 0.5, carbs 2.3, protein 3.7

Cream Pie with Lemon

Prep time: 20 minutes
Cooking time: 21 minutes
Servings: 8

Ingredients:

- 1 lemon
- 1 cup heavy cream
- 2 eggs
- 3 tablespoon butter
- 1 teaspoon baking soda
- 3 tablespoon coconut flour
- 1 ½ cup almond flour
- 2 teaspoon swerve
- 1 scoop stevia
- ¼ teaspoon salt

Directions:

Wash the lemon and slice it into the thin rings. Beat the eggs in the blender. Add heavy cream, butter, and baking soda. Blend it well on the maximum speed for 2 minutes. After this, add coconut flour, almond flour, swerve, and salt. Blend the mixture for 3 minutes more. The blended dough should be smooth but non-sticky. Preheat the air fryer to 300 F. Place the parchment in the air fryer dish. Roll the dough with the help of the rolling pin and transfer it to the air fryer dish. Then place the sliced lemon over the piecrust. Sprinkle the pie with the stevia. Cook the pie for 21 minutes. When the pie is cooked – chill it until the room temperature. Cut it into the servings. Taste it!

Nutrition: calories 247, fat 21.3, fiber 3.7, carbs 8.4, protein 6.7

Raspberry Cobbler

Prep time: 15 minutes
Cooking time: 10 minutes
Servings: 6

Ingredients:

- 1 cup raspberries
- 1 cup almond flour
- 1 tablespoon butter, melted
- 1 egg
- ½ teaspoon vanilla extract
- 2 teaspoon stevia powder

Directions:

Preheat the air fryer to 360 F. Slice and put the raspberries in the air fryer dish. Sprinkle the berries with 1 teaspoon of stevia powder. Combine the almond flour, butter, and vanilla extract in the bowl. Beat the egg in the almond flour and stir it carefully until homogenous. Then place the homogenous almond mixture over the sliced raspberries. Sprinkle the dough with the 1 teaspoon of the stevia powder. Put the cobbler in the air fryer dish. Cover the cobbler with the foil and make the X cut in the center of the foil. Then cook it for 10 minutes. If it is raw – cook it for 2-3 minutes more till it gets the doneness level. Cut the cobbler and serve. Enjoy!

Nutrition: calories 151, fat 11.7, fiber 3.4, carbs 6.8, protein 5.2

Vanilla-Cinnamon Cookies

Prep time: 15 minutes
Cooking time: 10 minutes
Servings: 14

Ingredients:
- 1 egg
- 1 tablespoon ground cinnamon
- 1 teaspoon vanilla extract
- 2 teaspoon swerve
- 1 scoop stevia powder
- 1 teaspoon baking soda
- 1 teaspoon apple cider vinegar
- 2 tablespoon coconut flour
- 1 cup almond flour
- 2 tablespoon heavy cream
- ¼ teaspoon salt
- 3 tablespoon butter

Directions:
Crack the egg in the blender and blend it until smooth. Then add ground cinnamon, vanilla extract, swerve, stevia powder, baking soda, and apple cider vinegar. Blend the mixture for 30 seconds. Then add coconut flour, almond flour, heavy cream, salt, and butter. Blend the mixture for 2 minutes. You will get the soft and elastic dough. Roll the dough and make the cookies from it with the help of the cutter. Preheat the air fryer to 355 F. Cover the air fryer dish with the parchment and put the cookies there. Cook the cookies for 10 minutes. Then let the cookies cool well. Enjoy!

Nutrition: calories 89, fat 7.5, fiber 1.6, carbs 3.2, protein 2.3

Pumpkin Bars

Prep time: 15 minutes
Cooking time: 10 minutes
Servings: 8

Ingredients:
- 6 tablespoon butter
- 6 tablespoon Erythritol
- 1 egg
- 10 drops liquid stevia
- ½ teaspoon ground ginger
- 1 cup pumpkin puree
- 2 tablespoon almond flour
- 2 tablespoon walnuts, crushed

Directions:
Melt the butter and combine it with the liquid stevia, Erythritol, ground ginger, almond flour, and crushed walnuts. Stir the mixture gently with the help of the spatula. Then beat the egg in the separate bowl and whisk it. Add the whisked egg in the almond flour mixture. Add pumpkin puree and mix it up. Roll the pumpkin dough with the help of the rolling pin and cut it into the bars. Preheat the air fryer to 365 F. Put the pumpkin bars in the air fryer and cook them for 10 minutes. The cooked pumpkin bars should be very soft. Chill the pumpkin bars. Enjoy!

Nutrition: calories 118, fat 11.3, fiber 1.2, carbs 14.4, protein 2

Flax Seed Muffins

Prep time: 15 minutes
Cooking time: 13 minutes
Servings: 8

Ingredients:

- 1 egg
- ½ cup butter
- 1 cup almond flour
- 1 teaspoon baking soda
- 1 tablespoon apple cider vinegar
- 1 teaspoon vanilla extract
- 3 tablespoon flax seeds
- 15 drops liquid stevia
- 1 teaspoon vanilla extract

Directions:

Beat the egg in the blender and blend it. Add butter and almond flour. Sprinkle the mixture with the baking soda and apple cider vinegar. Blend the mixture for 2 minutes. Add vanilla extract, flax seeds, liquid stevia, and vanilla extract. Blend the muffin mixture for 3 minutes on the medium speed. Preheat the air fryer to 350 F. Put the muffin dough into the muffin molds. Then place the muffin molds in the air fryer. Cook the muffins for 13 minutes. When the muffins are cooked – chill them. Enjoy!

Nutrition: calories 209, fat 19.5, fiber 2.2, carbs 3.9, protein 4.4

Avocado Pudding with Almond Flakes

Prep time: 20 minutes
Cooking time: 4 minutes
Servings: 6

Ingredients:

- ½ cup almond milk
- 2 avocado, pitted
- 1 teaspoon vanilla extract
- 7 drops liquid stevia
- 1 egg
- 3 tablespoon almond flakes
- 2 tablespoon butter
- ¼ teaspoon ground cinnamon

Directions:

Peel the avocado and chop it. Put the chopped avocado in the blender and blend it until you get a soft texture. Then beat the egg in the bowl and pour the almond milk. Add vanilla extract, liquid stevia, butter, and ground cinnamon. Mix it up with the help of the hand mixer. After this, preheat the air fryer to 250 F. Pour the almond milk mixture and cook it for 4 minutes. Stir the liquid every minute. After this, chill the almond milk liquid well. Pour the almond milk liquid into the blender with the smooth avocado. Blend it for 1 minute on the medium speed. Then pour the pudding into the glass vessels. Sprinkle the pudding with the almond flakes and keep in the fridge. Enjoy!

Nutrition: calories 247, fat 23.9, fiber 5.4, carbs 7.7, protein 3.3

Keto-Friendly Caramel

Prep time: 8 minutes
Cooking time: 6 minutes
Servings: 5

Ingredients:
- ½ cup butter, unsalted
- ¼ teaspoon salt
- ½ cup heavy cream
- 1 teaspoon Erythritol

Directions:
Preheat the air fryer to 350 F. Then toss the butter in the air fryer dish and melt it for 2 minutes. Then add salt and heavy cream. Stir the heavy cream with the help of the spatula until it is combined. Cook it for 3 minutes at the same temperature. Stir it every 1 minute. After this, add Erythritol and stir it well. Cook the caramel for 1 minute more. Then pour the cooked caramel in the glass vessel. Stir it frequently until the caramel is chill fully. Enjoy!

Nutrition: calories 204, fat 22.9, fiber 0, carbs 1.3, protein 0.4

Low Carb Chocolate Soufflé

Prep time: 15 minutes
Cooking time: 12 minutes
Servings: 6

Ingredients:
- 2 oz. dark chocolate, melted
- 5 tablespoon butter, unsalted
- 3 eggs, beaten
- 4 tablespoon Erythritol
- ¼ tablespoon vanilla extract
- 2 tablespoon almond flour
- 2 tablespoon heavy cream

Directions:
Separate the beaten eggs into the egg yolk and egg whites. Then melt the butter and combine it with the melted chocolate. Stir it. Whisk the egg yolk and combine it with Erythritol. Add the egg yolk mixture in the melted butter mixture. Add almond flour, vanilla extract, and heavy cream. Whisk it well. Then whisk the egg whites until you get the strong peaks. Add the egg whites to the chocolate mixture gradually. Stir it until homogenous. Pour the chocolate mixture into 6 ramekins. Preheat the air fryer to 330 F and put the ramekins there. Cook the soufflé for 12 minutes. Chill the cooked soufflé for 2 minutes. Taste it!

Nutrition: calories 200, fat 17.6, fiber 0.6, carbs 16.5, protein 4.2

Butter Pie

Prep time: 15 minutes
Cooking time: 20 minutes
Servings: 8

Ingredients:

- 1 teaspoon baking soda
- 1 tablespoon apple cider vinegar
- 1 cup almond flour
- ½ cup butter
- 1 egg
- 2 tablespoon Erythritol
- 1 teaspoon vanilla extract

Directions:

Melt the butter lightly. Combine the almond flour and baking soda. Add vanilla extract and Erythritol. Beat the egg in the bowl and whisk. Add the whisked egg in the almond flour. Then add the melted butter and apple cider vinegar. Knead the soft dough. Preheat the air fryer to 340 F. Cover the air fryer tray. Roll the dough with the help of the rolling pin in the size of the air fryer dish. Put the rolled dough in the air fryer and cook it for 20 minutes. When the pie is cooked – chill it and discard from the air fryer dish. Cut it into the servings. Serve the pie with the keto jam. Enjoy!

Nutrition: calories 196, fat 18.7, fiber 1.5, carbs 6.9, protein 3.8

Keto Cream Cheese Soufflé

Prep time: 15 minutes
Cooking time: 16 minutes
Servings: 7

Ingredients:

- 5 eggs
- 1 cup cream cheese
- 4 tablespoon heavy cream
- 6 tablespoon almond flour
- 4 tablespoon Erythritol
- 1 teaspoon coconut flakes

Directions:

Separate the eggs into the egg yolks and egg whites. Mix the egg yolks with Erythritol carefully. Add the cream cheese and almond flour. Mix the mass with the help of the hand mixer for 2 minutes at the maximum speed. Then add heavy cream and mix it up for 1 minute more. Whisk the egg whites until the strong peaks. Add the egg whites to the egg mixture slowly and stir it all the time. Combine the mixture with the coconut flakes. Preheat the air fryer to 330 F. Then pour the cream cheese mixture into 7 ramekins. Place the ramekins in the air fryer and cook for 16 minutes. When the soufflé is cooked – let it chill at the room temperature. Enjoy!

Nutrition: calories 227, fat 20.8, fiber 0.7, carbs 11.3, protein 7.9

Keto Donuts

Prep time: 15 minutes
Cooking time: 4 minutes
Servings: 8

Ingredients:
- 2 eggs
- ½ cup almond flour
- ¼ teaspoon salt
- ¼ teaspoon baking powder
- ½ teaspoon vanilla extract
- ¼ teaspoon ground ginger
- 1 tablespoon butter
- 2 tablespoon Erythritol
- 4 teaspoon heavy cream

Directions:
Crack the eggs in the blender and blend them. Add salt, baking powder, vanilla extract, and ground ginger. Blend it well. Then transfer the blended egg mixture into the mixing bowl. Add the almond flour, butter, Erythritol, and heavy cream. Knead the homogenous dough. If it is sticky – add more almond flour. Then roll the dough with the help of the rolling pin. Use the cutter to make the donuts. Preheat the air fryer to 350 F. Put the donuts in the air fryer basket. Cook the donuts for 4 minutes. When the donuts are cooked – transfer them to the serving plate. Enjoy!

Nutrition: calories 80, fat 6.8, fiber 0.8, carbs 5.6, protein 3

Keto Sweet Mini Rolls

Prep time: 20 minutes
Cooking time: 15 minutes
Servings: 6

Ingredients:
- 1 tablespoon ground cinnamon
- 3 tablespoon Erythritol
- 1 teaspoon baking powder
- 1 teaspoon fresh lemon juice
- 1 teaspoon lemon zest
- 1 cup almond flour
- 1 tablespoon coconut flakes
- 1 egg
- 1 pinch salt
- 1/3 cup heavy cream

Directions:
Combine the ground cinnamon and Erythritol. Then combine the baking powder, fresh lemon juice, lemon zest, and almond flour in the bowl. Add coconut flakes, salt, and heavy cream. Beat the egg in the separate bowl and whisk it. Then add the whisked egg in the almond flour mixture. Mix it up to make the homogenous dough. Roll the dough with the help of the rolling pin. Then sprinkle the surface of the dough with the ground cinnamon mixture. Roll it. Cut the roll into 6 parts. Preheat the air fryer to 350 F. Place the rolls in the air fryer and cook them for 15 minutes. When the rolls are cooked – check if they are cooked with the help of the toothpick. Chill the rolls. Enjoy!

Nutrition: calories 152, fat 12.4, fiber 2.7, carbs 13.3, protein 5.2

Vanilla Roll

Prep time: 25 minutes
Cooking time: 20 minutes
Servings: 10

Ingredients:
- 5 eggs
- ½ cup Erythritol
- 1 cup almond flour
- 1 tablespoon vanilla extract
- 1 pinch salt
- 1 cup heavy cream
- 2 scoop liquid stevia

Directions:

Beat the eggs and separate the egg yolks and egg whites. Then whisk the egg yolk with Erythritol. After this, combine the egg yolk mixture with the salt and almond flour. Stir it. Whisk the egg whites until the strong peaks. Add the egg whites to the egg yolk mixture. Add the vanilla extract. Stir it carefully. Preheat the air fryer to 290 F. Pour the dough in the air fryer dish and flatten it with the help of the spatula. Cook the meal for 20 minutes. After this, place the cooked pie in the wet towel. Whisk the heavy cream with the liquid stevia. When the heavy cream is thick – it is cooked. Spread the cooked dough with the whisked cream. Then roll it using the wet towel. Let the cooked roll rest for 10 minutes. Cut it into the servings. Enjoy!

Nutrition: calories 140, fat 12, fiber 1.2, carbs 14.9, protein 5.4

Hazelnut Balls

Prep time: 18 minutes
Cooking time: 8 minutes
Servings: 8

Ingredients:
- 2 tablespoon peanut butter
- 3 tablespoon Erythritol
- ½ teaspoon vanilla extract
- 1 cup almond flour
- 4 tablespoon hazelnuts, crushed
- ½ teaspoon baking soda
- 1 teaspoon apple cider vinegar

Directions:

Take the big mixing bowl and put the peanut butter there. Add Erythritol and stir it well. After this, add vanilla extract, almond flour, baking soda, and crushed hazelnuts. Knead the soft dough. Separate the dough into 8 pieces. Then roll the balls from the dough with the help of the fingertips. Preheat the air fryer to 360 F. Put the hazelnut balls in the air fryer and cook them for 8 minutes. When the balls are cooked – chill them well. Enjoy!

Nutrition: calories 123, fat 10.1, fiber 2, carbs 9.9, protein 4.4

Pumpkin Air Cookies

Prep time: 15 minutes
Cooking time: 8 minutes
Servings: 8

Ingredients:

- ½ cup pumpkin puree
- ¼ cup almond flour
- 1 tablespoon coconut flakes
- ½ teaspoon baking soda
- 3 tablespoon Erythritol
- 1 pinch salt
- 1 teaspoon ground cinnamon

Directions:

Combine the pumpkin puree with the almond flour. Then sprinkle the mixture with the coconut flakes, baking soda, Erythritol, salt, and ground cinnamon. Knead the smooth dough. If the dough is not smooth enough – add more almond flour. Roll the dough and use the cutter to make the cookies or separate it into 8 parts and roll the balls. After this, flatten the balls in the shape of cookies. Preheat the air fryer to 360 F. Put the cooked in the air fryer and cook them for 8 minutes. When the cookies are cooked – they will have crunchy edges but air center. Serve the cookies!

Nutrition: calories 29, fat 1.9, fiber 1, carbs 8, protein 1

Cashew Thin Pie

Prep time: 18 minutes
Cooking time: 18 minutes
Servings: 8

Ingredients:

- 1 egg
- 1 cup coconut flour
- 2 oz. cashews, crushed
- 1 oz. dark chocolate, melted
- 1/3 cup heavy cream
- ½ teaspoon baking soda
- 1 teaspoon apple cider vinegar
- 1 tablespoon butter

Directions:

Beat the egg in the blender and add coconut flour. After this, add melted chocolate, heavy cream, baking soda, apple cider vinegar, and butter. Blend it well. After this, transfer the dough to the bowl and sprinkle it with the crushed cashews. Knead the dough. Preheat the air fryer to 350 F. Place the dough in the air fryer dish and flatten it into the shape of the pie. Cook the pie for 18 minutes. When the pie is cooked – chill it well and only after this discard it from the dish. Cut it into the servings. Enjoy!

Nutrition: calories 158, fat 9.7, fiber 6.3, carbs 14.6, protein 4.2

Ricotta Mousse

Prep time: 20 minutes
Cooking time: 6 minutes
Servings: 4

Ingredients:
- 2 eggs
- ½ cup heavy cream
- 1 cup ricotta
- 3 tablespoon Erythritol
- 1 oz. butter
- 1 teaspoon vanilla extract

Directions:
Beat the eggs in the bowl and mix them with the help of the hand mixer. Then combine the mixed eggs with the heavy cream. Preheat the air fryer to 350 F. Pour the heavy cream mixture into the air fryer. Cook the liquid for 5 minutes. Stir the liquid every 1 minute. Then sprinkle the heavy cream mixture with the vanilla extract and stir it. Cook the liquid for 1 minute more. After this, pour the cooked heavy cream liquid in the bowl and whisk it for 4 minutes. When the liquid reaches the room temperature – add ricotta and butter. Mix it up for 1 minute more. Then place the cooked mousse in the glass vessels and keep in the fridge. Taste it!

Nutrition: calories 223, fat 18.4, fiber 0, carbs 15.2, protein 10.2

Keto Fudge

Prep time: 15 minutes
Cooking time: 1 minute
Servings: 3

Ingredients:
- ½ cup heavy cream
- ½ cup butter
- 1 teaspoon ground cinnamon
- 15 drops liquid stevia
- 1 pinch salt

Directions:
Melt the butter and combine it with the ground cinnamon. Add the heavy cream and liquid stevia. After this, add salt and mix the mixture using the hand mixer. Preheat the air fryer to 360 F. Pour the whisked mixture into the air fryer and cook it for 1 minute. Then pour the mixture into the bowl and chill it for 10 minutes. After this, whisk it for 1 minute and place in the fridge. When the fudge is solid – it is cooked. Enjoy!

Nutrition: calories 299, fat 32.9, fiber 0.4, carbs 1.9, protein 0.7

Delightful Custard

Prep time: 10 minutes
Cooking time: 28 minutes
Servings: 4

Ingredients:

- 5 eggs
- ½ cup cream cheese
- ½ cup water
- 1 teaspoon vanilla extract
- 2 tablespoon Erythritol

Directions:

Preheat the air fryer to 320 F. Beat the eggs in the mixing bowl and whisk them. Then add the cream cheese and water. Whisk it well for 2 minutes. After this, add vanilla extract and Erythritol. Stir it until homogenous. Pour the mixture into the ramekins and transfer in the air fryer. Cook the custard for 28 minutes. When the custard is cooked – let it chill well. Enjoy!

Nutrition: calories 183, fat 15.6, fiber 0, carbs 8.8, protein 9.1

Nuts Fudge

Prep time: 10 minutes
Cooking time: 3 minutes
Servings: 8

Ingredients:

- ½ cup peanut butter
- ½ cup macadamia nuts
- ¼ cup cream cheese
- 1 teaspoon vanilla extract
- 3 tablespoon Erythritol

Directions:

Preheat an air fryer to 360 F. Place the peanut butter in the air fryer dish. Add vanilla extract and Erythritol. Stir it. Cook the mass for 3 minutes. After this, remove the peanut butter mixture from the air fryer and stir it for 3 minutes. Add cream cheese and whisk it. Place the prepared fudge mixture on the tray and flatten it. Freeze it until solid. Then cut the fudge into 8 parts. Enjoy!

Nutrition: calories 182, fat 17, fiber 1.7, carbs 10.2, protein 5.2

Strawberry Grated Pie

Prep time: 25 minutes
Cooking time: 25 minutes
Servings: 8

Ingredients:

- ½ cup strawberry, chopped
- 1 cup almond flour
- 1 tablespoon coconut flour
- 1 pinch salt
- 4 tablespoon Erythritol
- ½ teaspoon baking soda
- 1 teaspoon apple cider vinegar
- 1/3 cup butter
- ¼ teaspoon ground nutmeg

Directions:

Combine the almond flour, coconut flour, salt, Erythritol, baking soda, apple cider vinegar, butter, and ground nutmeg in the mixing bowl. Knead the homogenous dough. Place the dough in the fridge for 10 minutes. After this, preheat the air fryer to 350 F. Grate the dough. Separate the grated dough into 2 parts. Then place the first part of the grated dough in the air fryer dish. Sprinkle it with the chopped strawberry. Then cover it with the second part of the grated dough. Put the pie in the air fryer and cook for 25 minutes. When the pie is cooked – chill it. After this, discard the pie from the air fryer and slice it into servings. Enjoy!

Nutrition: calories 159, fat 14.5, fiber 2.1, carbs 11.9, protein 3.3

Rhubarb Bars

Prep time: 15 minutes
Cooking time: 8 minutes
Servings: 6

Ingredients:

- ½ cup rhubarb
- ¼ cup Erythritol
- ¼ teaspoon ground ginger
- ½ cup coconut flour
- 3 tablespoon heavy cream
- 1 teaspoon vanilla extract
- 1 tablespoon butter

Directions:

Blend the rhubarb and combine it with Erythritol and ground ginger. Add coconut flour and heavy cream. After this, add vanilla extract and butter. Knead the soft dough. Roll the dough and cut it into 6 squares. Preheat the air fryer to 350 F. Place the rhubarb squares in the air fryer and cook for 8 minutes. Chill the cooked bars. Enjoy!

Nutrition: calories 87, fat 3.6, fiber 4.2, carbs 16.2, protein 1.6

Peanut Butter Cups with Coconut

Prep time: 30 minutes
Cooking time: 4 minutes
Servings: 5

Ingredients:

- 1/3 cup coconut milk
- 2 tablespoon coconut flakes
- 2 tablespoon butter, melted
- 5 tablespoon peanut butter
- 3 tablespoon almond flour
- 1 pinch salt
- ½ teaspoon vanilla extract

Directions:

Combine the peanut butter and almond flour together. Add salt and vanilla extract. Knead the dough, Take the ramekins. Cut the dough into 5 parts. Place the dough in the ramekins in the shape of the piecrust. Preheat the air fryer to 360 F and cook the piecrust for 4 minutes. Combine the coconut milk and coconut flakes. Add butter and mix it up with the help of the hand mixer. Put the coconut milk mixture in the freezer and chill it for at least 10 minutes. When the piecrust ramekins are cooked – chill them well. Pour the coconut milk mixture into the cooked pie crust. Serve the meal or keep it in the fridge. Enjoy!

Nutrition: calories 205, fat 19.1, fiber 1.9, carbs 5.3, protein 5.4

Blackberry Tart

Prep time: 20 minutes
Cooking time: 25 minutes
Servings: 8

Ingredients:

- ½ cup blackberry
- 1/3 cup Erythritol
- 1 cup almond flour
- 4 tablespoon butter
- 1 pinch salt
- 1 teaspoon vanilla extract
- 2 tablespoon coconut flour
- 1 egg

Directions:

Combine the blackberries with Erythritol. Stir the mixture carefully. Beat the egg in the bowl and whisk it. Add almond flour and salt. Then sprinkle the mixture with the butter, vanilla extract, and coconut flour. Knead the dough. Preheat the air fryer to 355 F. Cover the air fryer dish with the parchment, Roll the dough with the help of the rolling pin. Place the rolled dough in the air fryer dish. Place the blackberries over the dough. Cook the tart for 25 minutes. When the tart is cooked – chill it. Cut it into servings. Taste it!

Nutrition: calories 156, fat 13.2, fiber 2.7, carbs 15.2, protein 4.1

Conclusion

The ketogenic diet (Keto Diet) is a perfect way not just losing the weight but also to keep your body in shape. There are many benefits of this diet such as normalizing of the hunger, controlling the blood pressure and the cholesterol level.

Sometimes Keto diet can maintain the normal condition of the human's organism during epilepsy.

Such problem as acne can be also solved while following such way of eating. You can find that some people use Keto diet as a lifestyle. Otherwise, it can be dangerous and can damage your health. There is a doctor's recommendation to start the diet from 7 days; after this, you should make a small gap. If you change all your diet fast – the organism will have shock and you will not get that desired effect.

This book will help you to learn how to cook the keto dishes in an easy and fast way. The best, delightful, and easy recipes that do not need special ingredients will make your dinner, lunch, breakfast, and even snack very tasty. You can be sure that air fryer and the recipes of this book will turn your imagination about food and diets! Try the keto dishes and you will make the holiday for your family and friends everyday!

Recipe Index

Made in the USA
Middletown, DE
08 January 2018